let's sew together

simple projects the whole family can make

rubyellen bratcher

POTTER
CRAFT

new york

Copyright © 2014 by Rubyellen Bratcher

Published in the United States by Potter Craft, an imprint of Crown Publishing Group,
a division of Random House, LLC, a Penguin Random House Company, New York.

www.pottercraft.com
www.crownpublishing.com

POTTER CRAFT and colophon are registered trademarks of Random House, LLC.

Library of Congress Cataloging-in-Publication Data
Bratcher, Rubyellen N.
  Let's sew together! : simple projects the whole family can make /
Rubyellen N. Bratcher.—First edition.
       pages cm
1. Sewing. 2. House furnishings. 3. Dress accessories. I. Title.
  TT705.B73 2014
  646.2—dc23   2013019030

ISBN 978-0-385-34518-7
eBook ISBN 978-0-385-34519-4

Printed in China

Book and cover design by Ashley Tucker
Cover photographs by Rubyellen Bratcher

Photography on the following pages by Kimberly Geneviève:
3, 4, 68, 80, 85, 37 (bottom right), 118
All other photography and illustrations by Rubyellen Bratcher
Additional artwork by True and Brave Bratcher
Styling on the following pages by Heather Rome: 38, 42, 48, 62, 73, 97, 134, 142

10 9 8 7 6 5 4 3 2 1
First Edition

Ben, **True**, **Brave**,
Soul, and **Glow**,
this book is for you.

contents

introduction

My adventures in sewing began on an ordinary day of shopping in downtown Glendora, when I wandered into the cutest baby boutique. I had just had my first child, and my heart fluttered when I saw so many pretty, girly clothes and toys. Then I turned over the price tag on a tiny skirt, and my heart sank. There was no way that I would be able to afford it. When our baby was born, I retired from teaching to be a stay-at-home mom, and my husband, just out of grad school, was starting a new job. But in that boutique, instead of feeling disappointed, I got an idea: we needed a sewing machine.

When I got home, I figured out how much money our family could save by investing in a sewing machine. (Compared to the prices in that boutique, we would save a *lot* of money.) My husband, being the practical man that he is, saw the many benefits of home sewing and agreed. Or maybe I just bugged him to death until he caved. Either way, he loves me and could see how badly I wanted to make our little girl all the sweet little clothes, toys, and room decorations she deserved.

Before we made the big purchase, I signed up for sewing lessons at a local fabric shop. For the first lesson, the instructor asked what I wanted to make. She taught me a few basic techniques, including how to thread the machine and stitch a straight line, and I came home with exactly what I had wanted: a nursing cover and a tiny, adorable baby skirt. Two sewing projects that I had only imagined in my head had come to life in front of me! I was one step closer to my goal, and my heart started fluttering again. After a lot of research, I finally bought the machine I wanted from a local shop, took it home, and haven't stopped sewing since. When I finished my month of sewing lessons at the first shop, I continued with a series of lessons at another. They taught me the essentials, but I learned even more from the time I spent at home, behind my machine. When in doubt, I simply needed to sew, sew, and sew some more.

Since those early days when I first fell in love with sewing, it has only gotten sweeter with time. Our family has grown to include four little girls who love to get involved with my sewing projects—or should I say *our* sewing projects. They often decide what we should sew and exactly how they want it. I let them have a say in the color and fabric and allow them the freedom to add whatever details, embellishments, or surface decorations they choose. Our family's craft time is all about working together and having fun.

Collaborative crafting means not only sewing for but also sewing with your kids. No matter their ages, your children can have a hand in sewing with you. After all, sewing is just a fancier way of playing connect-the-dots. It's about following lines and shapes, skills that kids are already practicing as they learn to draw and write. As with drawing and writing, once they get the basics of sewing, only their imaginations will limit them. Sewing with your kids involves a certain degree of skill, but more important, it's about collaboration. Allow everyone to contribute something, and you'll make lasting memories. Let them be involved, and they'll experience how much fun it is to make something with their own hands.
Kids learn a great deal from observing, so even if you end up doing most of the sewing, let them sit next to you and watch. You may be amazed by the knowledge they pick up!

A few of the easy projects

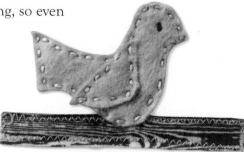

in this book require nothing more than a straight stitch to create a simple dress or a picnic blanket for family outings. Other projects involve a bit more attention to detail or special techniques such as embroidery or quilting, but you'll find that they're totally achievable with the right guidance. In some of the more time-intensive projects, you'll find tips to simplify them. There's no pressure to make perfectly sewn projects here. Uneven stitches and crooked lines only add to the charm of a handmade item.

I am a mom, and I totally get it. You have kids to teach, laundry waiting, meals to cook, and an endless schedule of dance and sports practices. But you also dream of making something that will brighten your day. Each chapter in this book is dedicated to a particular aspect of daily life and family routines. Whether you're a spontaneous parent or one who likes to plan, this book offers something for you and your child. If he or she doesn't feel like sewing, use the sidebars to find reading suggestions, learning activities, and playtime ideas. All the projects in this book will fit into your busy family schedule and show you that sewing is truly magical.

Have fun with the projects and let them reflect your family's personal style. I am so grateful to have the opportunity to write this book and share some of our creations, but this is now your creation, too. Sewing is like magic, and you have the ability to create it yourself. I know there are some of you out there who have a sewing machine but may be too intimidated to start. *Let's Sew Together* is here to help you find the time and encouragement to try those projects you've always wanted to make. And you will be sewing with your little ones every chance you get! Let's take it one stitch at a time.

let's start sewing!

how to use this book

This chapter will introduce you to some basic tools, tips, and tricks for sewing. Sewing is much easier than you think!

SKILL LEVELS I think everyone has the magic sewing touch, so don't let a project that has a lot of steps scare you. I don't like to say that a project is difficult, because I think anything can be done, even if it takes longer. Look out for these icons to help guide you to a project that works for the amount of time you have on hand.

SEW QUICK: ☺ Using one basic sewing technique, these projects can be whipped up rather quickly.

MAKE IN AN AFTERNOON: ☺☺ These projects use a few more sewing techniques or require assembling multiple pattern pieces.

TAKE YOUR TIME: ☺☺☺ Don't let anything hold you back from trying these projects, too. Just slow down and pay attention to all the pattern pieces and their placement. These projects utilize a variety of techniques and may take more than just an afternoon to complete.

NO-SEW: These are quick little projects with items you probably have around the house already. No sewing necessary—just imagination, a good attitude, and perhaps some paper and paint.

PATTERNS Some projects also have patterns that need to be enlarged and printed out. But who has a copy machine sitting around the house? If you're pressed for time or resources, just redraw the template on a large sheet of paper based on the dimensions of the patterns in this book.

the sewing machine

First, let me introduce you to one of my good friends . . . my sewing machine! You can sew anything by hand, but if you have children, this device will scratch that creative itch and save a lot of time. There are many brands and models on the market, so my advice is to think about the types of sewing that interest you (basic sewing,

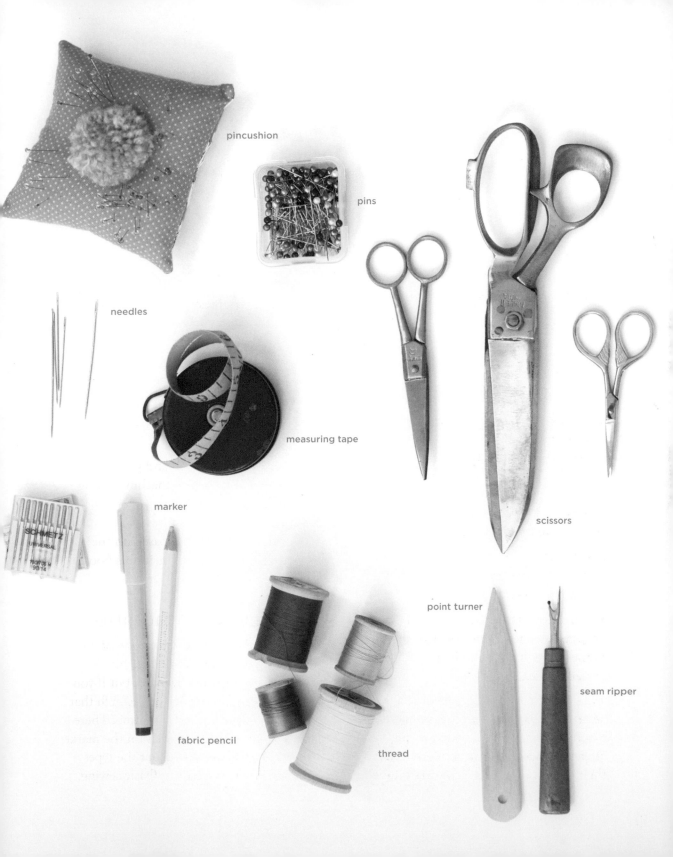

pincushion

pins

needles

measuring tape

marker

scissors

fabric pencil

thread

point turner

seam ripper

quilting, or maybe embroidery), and then visit a local sewing shop. Talk with the staff, let them know your skill level, and give the machines a test drive. You'll know which one feels right for you.

Most machines these days have a friendly automatic threader. If yours does, use it to your heart's delight. It's the best little contraption ever. Before threading the machine's needle, don't forget to follow the guidelines that show where to place the thread and wind it around the machine properly. If it's threaded incorrectly, the machine won't sew.

Sewing machine manuals are also a wonderful resource and will answer many of the basic questions. We typically ignore manuals that come with electronic devices, but you'll want to keep your sewing machine manual somewhere convenient so you can refer to it again and again.

basic sewing supplies

Before you start using a sewing machine, I recommend having the following supplies on hand. The projects in this book call for "basic sewing supplies," and organizing them in your sewing area (or cramming them in a box) makes your crafting time that much easier. Instead of spending time hunting for these necessities, you can spend more time making. As a parent, I know how fast the days go by, and there really isn't much downtime. I want you to be able to use your time more efficiently when you are given the opportunity to create.

SCISSORS I use a nice pair of 8" (20.5cm) dressmaking shears with sharp blades that can cut through layers of fabric. For fine details like clipping corners and snipping threads, I use a small pair of embroidery scissors. The number-one rule is to use nice fabric scissors *only* for fabric.

---

sewing machine 101

Just as you would get a car regularly oiled and checked, make sure to properly maintain your sewing machine. A clean and well-oiled machine will serve you for many years, its stitch tension will be better regulated, and the stitches will be more even. Local sewing or craft shops stock lubricating oil specially made for sewing machines, and always check the manual for specific maintenance instructions.

Never use them to cut paper or anything else because the blades will dull. I keep another pair of 8" (20.5cm) scissors around for everything else, including cutting patterns and templates. Fabric scissors and everyday scissors should always be clearly distinguishable from each other. Make sure your children know that there are different scissors for different purposes by adding a unique mark, such as a labeled band of washi tape, around the handle.

IRON AND IRONING BOARD An iron is just as important as a sewing machine. Keep an iron and an ironing board within arm's reach so you can press fabrics and seams as you work.

SEWING MACHINE NEEDLES I use a universal needle for most sewing projects and replace it with a denim needle for heavyweight fabrics or multiple layers of fabric. Always switch out the needle based on the type of fabric you are going to sew.

ASSORTED HAND-SEWING NEEDLES Hand-sewing needles vary in length and sharpness, so choose the right one depending on the type of project you are working on.

SHARPS: Medium-length needles are most commonly used for hand-sewing. This is the type I use for most of my hand-sewing needs.

EMBROIDERY NEEDLES: Similar to sharps, embroidery needles have longer eyes suitable for threading embroidery floss.

APPLIQUÉ NEEDLES: Short, thin needles work well with smaller stitches and fine, detailed work like appliqué.

QUILTING NEEDLES: With rounded eyes, these shorter needles allow you to sew quickly and accurately. Just as their name suggests, they are ideal for quilting.

PLASTIC SEWING OR LACING NEEDLES Child-friendly oversize needles have dull points, larger eyes, and thicker bodies,

stay sharp!

Change your needles often! Needles dull much more quickly than you think and need to be changed frequently. Some people recommend replacing the needle after every project, but if I did that, all my money would go to buying new needles. My experience is that at least once a week is sufficient.

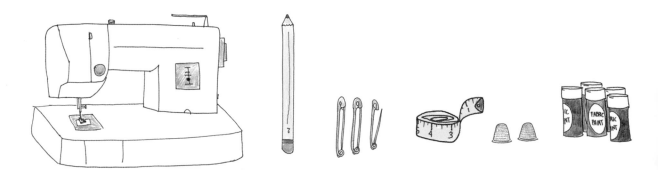

making them perfect for little hands to practice hand-sewing. Keep a handful of them around for simple sewing projects.

FABRIC PENCIL, AIR-FADING MARKER, AND/OR TAILOR'S CHALK Use any of these tools to mark fabric when cutting or altering. Fabric pencil and tailor's chalk come off easily just by erasing the pencil markings or brushing off the chalk dust. My personal favorite is an air-fading marker because the marks disappear on their own.

MEASURING TAPE A pliable fabric or plastic tape measures curved items and body shapes.

PINS Keep a variety of all-purpose pins and glass-head pins at the ready. All-purpose pins are good for general sewing, while the glass heads allow you to iron on pinned  areas without fear of melting them. Most of the time, I use glass-head pins because I iron projects frequently as I sew.

PINCUSHION Give your pins a home to keep little feet (or big ones, for that matter) from stepping on them. You can make a beginner's pincushion later in this chapter (page 31).

POINT TURNER This tool helps turn projects inside out, pop out corners, and crease seams. If I can't find mine, I use the end of a paintbrush or a chopstick. Any of them gets the job done.

ASSORTED THREAD Thread is a big deal. If you want to hide the line of stitching, choose a color that matches the fabric (or

the most dominant color in a print). If you want the stitches to stand out, choose a contrasting color. Your projects are *your* projects, so choose thread based on whichever look appeals to you.

ALL-PURPOSE COTTON/BLENDED THREAD: Best for hand- and machine-sewing, this medium-weight thread works well with many fabrics. I sew mostly with blended all-purpose thread because it's much more durable than cotton.

QUILTING THREAD: Heavier than all-purpose thread, it's best used for hand-quilting. It will tangle if used in machine-quilting.

HEAVY-DUTY THREAD: This is used for upholstery or thick fabrics like denim.

SEAM RIPPER This tool is the sewing version of an eraser, with a hook and sharp edge that can easily cut stitches so they can be removed. As you're learning, it will be your new best friend.

SEAM GAUGE This is a ruler with an adjustable marker that helps keep seams even while pinning, marking fabric, or sewing. The marker moves to the determined seam allowance.

fabric

Your choice can make all the difference and help your project shine. These are a few of my favorite types of fabric.

COTTON: Most projects in the book use cotton fabrics. I love cotton because it is so soft and natural.

LINEN: Linen is fabulous because it drapes well and feels comfortable close to the skin. I prefer to make clothes out of linen.

HEAVYWEIGHT FABRIC: I use it in some of the home decor projects in this book.

WOOL AND WOOL FELT: Kids especially love using this fabric in craft projects because it requires no hemming and can be used for fun, easy embellishments.

OILCLOTH: Great for quick and easy projects, the edges don't need to be finished or hemmed. Two projects in the book (pages 91 and 155) use chalk cloth, a type of oilcloth that can be drawn on with chalk. Use a rolling foot (Sewing Machine Feet, page 16) when sewing on oilcloth or chalk cloth.

FABRIC CARE Wash and press all fabrics before sewing with them. Ideally, you should check the selvedge of the fabrics for care instructions, but I'll admit that I don't always follow this rule. To compensate for the shrinkage that may occur, I typically add ½" (13mm) to the seams. But with prewashed fabrics, just follow the directions word for word.

FABRIC EMBELLISHMENT Even with all the choices out there, you might not find the perfect fabric for a project. Don't be afraid to test out new waters: if you can't find a print you like, just make it! My favorite way to design fabric is to have my kids draw or paint on it. Kids always create without overthinking, so the designs they come up with look natural.

When using fabric markers or fabric paint, place the fabric in a single layer on top of cardboard or a stack of scrap paper. Otherwise, the color may bleed through and end up somewhere unexpected.

FABRIC MARKERS: Fabric markers come in a wide variety of colors. Once the design is complete, the image must be heat-set with an iron. Some brands of markers may have different instructions on how to set them, so make sure to follow their directions.

FABRIC PAINT: Use specially formulated fabric paint, or use acrylic paint mixed with a little bit of fabric medium. Fabric paint gives a thinner consistency, whereas acrylic paint mixed with fabric medium makes the painted areas slightly thicker. Always allow images to dry completely and heat-set to make them permanent.

IRON-ON TRANSFERS: For smaller-scale projects, photocopy a favorite image onto iron-on transfer paper, then iron the image onto fabric, following the manufacturer's instructions. Use pictures of loved ones, landscapes, or your child's original artwork.

where to find fabric?

Part of the fun of sewing is choosing fabric. Local fabric shops offer a million choices, but vintage linens and bedsheets from thrift stores work just as well. Don't be shy about cutting up old clothes with unusual patterns to reuse in projects.

optional (but recommended) tools

These are additional tools and gadgets that I like to have on hand. I am, admittedly, a bit of a craft hoarder, but I've found that these extras are very well worth the investment.

BIAS TAPE MAKER Handy and dandy, this little guy helps create bias tape by folding strips of fabric as you iron. Making your own bias tape will give you endless possibilities compared to the limited selection in stores.

CLEAR PLASTIC SEWING AND QUILTING RULER To mark or cut straight lines on fabric, use a clear plastic quilting ruler. Pair it with a rotary cutter and self-healing mat, and you will feel like a pro!

EMBROIDERY HOOP A circular frame that keeps fabric taut for embroidery or other needlework, it's great to use for ease and stability when teaching children the basics of hand-sewing, too.

PENCIL (WITH AN ERASER) Use it to lightly mark fabric or paper patterns.

PINKING SHEARS To prevent fabric from unraveling, use these scissors to cut zigzag edges. They are commonly used as a quick way to finish off inseams (page 25).

ROTARY CUTTER AND SELF-HEALING MAT
These two tools go hand in hand and make cutting a lot quicker with straighter and cleaner edges.

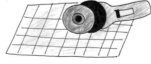

SAFETY PINS I use these to pull a strip of fabric right side out, or to pull elastic, ribbon, cording, or drawstrings through casings. You can also use a specially designed bodkin.

SEWING MACHINE FEET Having a variety of feet on hand makes certain tasks easier. I recommend investing in a zipper foot, free-motion quilting foot, rolling foot, and buttonhole foot.

THIMBLE Worn on your middle finger, a thimble protects you from getting calloused, poked, and prodded when hand-sewing. Your skin will thank you.

YARDSTICK Use it to measure and make long straight edges that can't be drawn with a standard ruler.

machine-sewing

You'll use the following basic stitches for most of the projects you want to make. The most important (and easiest) skill is sewing a simple straight line.

As you're sewing, keep your eye on the guide (called the *throat plate*), not on the needle itself. The throat plate is located just under your sewing machine's needle. Set the speed of the stitching to a moderate pace, so you can keep an eye on the guide and keep the line of stitching straight. Many times, I have rushed through a project and ended up taking longer because I was not keeping my eye on the guide, or was creating crooked or poorly placed stitches that had to be ripped out. Like the fable of the tortoise and the hare, slow and steady wins the race.

PINNING FABRIC Before you begin sewing (by machine or hand), pin the fabric to help prevent movement. It does take some time, but it is always time well spent.

1 Lay the fabric pieces on a flat surface and line up the edges of the seam and fabric.

2 Place pins perpendicular to the raw edge of the fabric about 5" (12.5cm) apart (or closer for smaller projects) for the entire length of the seam.

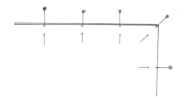

STRAIGHT STITCH This is the most commonly used stitch. The same technique is used to topstitch and edge stitch, just by adjusting the fabric and placement of stitching. A straight stitch is used for joining fabrics, hemming, and finishing folded edges. Short stitches (1mm–3mm, or 9–24 stitches per inch) are used for lightweight and delicate fabrics, medium-length stitches (2.5mm–3mm, or 9–13 stitches per inch) for general sewing, and long stitches (4mm–6mm, or 4–6 stitches per inch) for basting or sewing with heavyweight fabrics like oilcloth.

I am a firm believer that the key to unlocking the magic in sewing is sewing a straight seam. Once you can do that, you will step into a whole new world of possibility. All you need to do is follow these simple steps:

1 With the right sides of the fabric together, pin the fabric at evenly spaced intervals with the pins perpendicular to the seam. Typical seam allowances are between ¼" (6mm) and ½" (13mm), but refer to the project's instructions.

2 Place the fabric under the needle, lower the presser foot, and go. Make sure to backstitch the first couple of stitches by holding down the reverse button on the sewing machine to secure the stitching in place. There is no need to push or pull the fabric through; the machine will do that for you. Your job is to keep a steady pace and feed the fabric through so that it lines up with the guide. Natural tendency is to watch the needle when stitching, but to ensure straight lines, watch the throat plate and presser foot. The marks on the throat plate serve as a guide for the seam allowance.

3 When the line of stitching is finished, backstitch the last couple of stitches. Raise the needle to its highest position and lift the presser foot. Pull the fabric away from the needle and cut the threads. Snip any excess threads as close to the last stitch as possible.

EDGE STITCH This is simply a straight stitch that is sewn close to the edge. Typically, the line of stitching is ⅛"–⅕" (3mm–6mm) away from the folded edge.

TOPSTITCH A visible, decorative straight line of stitching adds a professional finishing touch. Stitch with the right side of the fabric facing up and choose a slightly longer stitch length. The key to topstitching is wonderfully straight lines, so practice really does make perfect here.

ZIGZAG STITCH This stitch is used for attaching appliqués, making buttonholes, and attaching trim and elastic, or for finishing off seams (page 25). Choose the width of the zigzag necessary for coverage; the smaller the number, the less of a zigzag (i.e., setting the stitch width to 0 produces almost a straight stitch), and a higher setting provides a wider zigzag. Setting the stitch length smaller creates a close zigzag, whereas a higher number makes the zigzag more open. Most machines have zigzag settings built in. For example, an appliqué requires a higher-setting zigzag in width, but choose a closer setting in length to be sure to fully enclose the appliqué. Also, when using the zigzag stitch for an appliqué, the foot has to be placed on the edge of the appliqué for the needle to zigzag-stitch right on the edge.

basic hand-sewing

I sewed my first baby dress all by hand. No sewing machine at all. Though they do take more time, basic hand-sewing techniques definitely come in handy.

THREADING A NEEDLE With practice, it's surprisingly easy to thread a hand-sewing needle the proper way without even needing a needle threader.

1 Cut a piece of thread about an arm's length, plus a few extra inches. Snip the end of the thread at a 45-degree angle. This gives the thread a sharp edge.

2 Hold the needle upright and slightly tilted, so that you can see the eye clearly.

With your other hand, push at least ½" (13mm) of thread through the eye. If it doesn't go through, rub a little soap at the end (or lick it) and try to feed it through the hole again.

3 Once the thread is on the other side, pull the thread through the eye.

4 Loop the thread around the tip of your index finger to prepare to tie a knot at the end. For a thicker knot, loop the thread around your finger a few more times.

5 Roll the thread loop off your fingertip, keeping the thread taut, and with the loop of thread pinched between your thumb and finger, pull it down into a knot.

FINISHING KNOT As in machine-sewing, a backstitch secures the line of stitching.

1 Take one small backstitch (page 20) at the end and make a loop over the point of the needle.

2 Pull the thread through the loop to create a knot at the base of the fabric.

3 Repeat again to secure the stitch.

BURYING THE TAILS This simple trick hides thread tails in a project after the thread has been knotted.

1 Once the line of sewing is finished, knot the last stitch (step 5, above).

2 Insert the needle into the fabric and pull the thread so that it tightens a bit.

3 Pull out the needle and trim the thread as close as possible to the fabric. The tails of the thread will be buried inside the fabric.

RUNNING STITCH Simple and quick, this is the same technique used when basting by hand. (Basting is a long stitch used to hold fabrics together temporarily.) Running stitches (and basting) are easy to take out once the permanent stitches are set in place. These can also be used when test-fitting a garment or attaching a zipper.

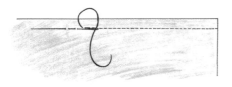

1 Thread the needle and knot the tail end. Insert the needle from the wrong side and into the right side of the fabric at evenly spaced intervals.

2 Continue to pull the needle and thread through the wrong side and into the right side of the fabric until the desired length of stitching is reached.

3 When the line or curve is finished, end with the needle at the back of the work.

4 Thread the needle back and forth through the back of the stitches to secure.

BLANKET STITCH This stitch is both decorative and functional, used on edges.

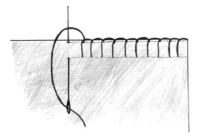

1 Thread the needle and knot the tail end. Insert the needle from the back of the fabric, about ¼" (6mm) from the edge.

2 Insert the needle up through the wrong side of the fabric again, creating a loop around the fabric edge.

3 Insert the needle under the previous loop stitch (the needle will be perpendicular to the fabric edge). The thread is now held in place. To complete one blanket stitch, insert the needle down into the right side of the fabric, lining it up with the previous loop, and pull it up through the loop of thread.

4 Continue from step 3 for consecutive stitches. End with a finishing knot and bury the tails.

SLIP STITCH Use this stitch to close pillows and softies, creating an invisible seam.

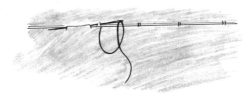

1 Insert the needle through the fold of a fabric and anchor the stitch with a knot inside the fold.

2 Point the needle to the left, gather a few threads of fabric onto the needle close to the edge of the hem, and insert the needle directly below the stitch through the fabric.

3 Insert the needle horizontally through the folded edge and pull it out the same distance as the previous stitch.

4 Insert the needle again and then cross horizontally the same distance as the previous stitch. Pass directly down through the folded edge, and insert the needle again into the fold. Repeat from step 2 for the desired length. End with a finishing knot and bury the tails.

embroidery techniques

Embroidery stitches are a great way to add details or a little bit of oomph to a project.

USING AN EMBROIDERY HOOP

The most essential item when embroidering by hand is a hoop.

1 Transfer or draw a design on fabric.

2 Place the area of the fabric to embroider inside the hoop and secure.

3 Insert the needle from the wrong side to the right side and stitch the design using one of the following stitches.

---

no embroidery hoop?

You can also hold the fabric taut with your hands if an embroidery hoop isn't available.

BACKSTITCH In addition to outlining embroidered designs, this strong reinforcing stitch can be used to join two pieces of fabric. Remember, the stitch moves backward before it goes forward.

1 Insert the needle from the wrong side of the fabric, up through the right side.

2 Bring the needle back down through the right side. Pull the thread through.

3 Come back up through the wrong side of the fabric at a distance equal to the previous stitch and then insert the needle in the spot it first came out of, and pull the thread through. This is the first backstitch. Continue from step 1 for the desired length. Weave in the ends through the stitches on the wrong side to secure.

SATIN STITCH This stitch is often used for filling in an image as the stitches are placed very closely together. I usually outline a design with backstitch and fill in the shapes with satin stitch.

1 Insert the needle from the wrong side, coming up through the right side at an angle.

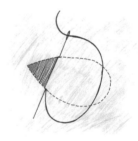

2 Insert the needle down through the right side and up from the wrong side at an angle. Repeat this step until the design is filled in.

CROSS-STITCH This stitch is ideal for linen or burlap where the weave of the fabric is clearly visible and provides a graph for cross-stitching.

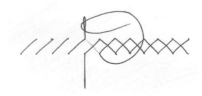

1 Insert the needle from the wrong side of the fabric and create a row of evenly spaced diagonal lines on the right side.

2 Reverse the direction of stitching and cross each diagonal line with another diagonal line in the opposite direction. Bring the needle in and out of the same holes where the Xs meet.

beyond the basics

Now that you've got your stitches down, it's time to put it all together! These techniques are used in different projects sprinkled throughout the book. I recommend practicing on a piece of scrap fabric before you apply a new technique to a project. It takes time to build a repertoire of sewing skills, and sometimes you may learn the most from your mistakes with scrap fabric.

TURNING ON A STRAIGHT STITCH

1 At the corner (still observing your seam allowance), pause at the corner point, leaving the needle down in the fabric.

2 Raise the presser foot and pivot to follow the corner. Drop the presser foot and continue stitching.

Another option is to sew a straight stitch off the fabric in one direction, then turn the fabric to go in the other direction and straight stitch again. This provides a stronger corner seam. Before turning the piece right side out, clip the corner at a 45-degree angle to reduce bulk. Be careful not to snip the actual stitching. When turning, use a point turner to help pop out the corners and make them sharp.

SEWING CURVES When sewing a curve, go slowly and do not pull on the fabric or you might distort the intended shape. After a curve is sewn, clip Vs evenly along the curve (Clipping Corners and Curves, below), being mindful not to clip the stitching. If at any point you need to lift the presser foot, make sure the needle is down in the fabric before lifting the presser foot.

clipping corners and curves

Working with smaller scissors gives you more control. Clip around convex (outer) curves with V shapes spaced at even intervals. Clip concave (inner) curves with straight lines perpendicular to the line of stitching. Clip corners at a 45-degree angle. Always be careful not to get too snippy and clip the actual stitching!

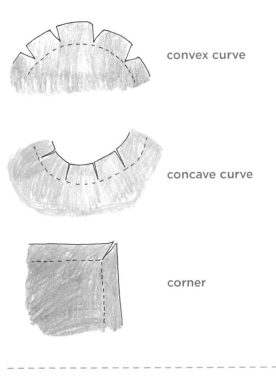

convex curve

concave curve

corner

TURNING ON A ZIGZAG STITCH

1 Sew a straight line of stitching. At the point you need to turn or curve (and still observing the seam allowance), when the needle is on the outside of the edge of the fabric, pause and leave the needle down in the fabric.

2 Raise the presser foot and pivot to follow the corner or curve. Drop the presser foot down and continue the zigzag stitch. This tip works well for other decorative stitches, too.

APPLIQUÉ You will need a piece of fusible web and a pencil, in addition to basic sewing supplies (page 12) to appliqué a motif. For projects with heavier fabrics, you can omit the fusible web.

1 Place the fusible web directly over the template for the motif with the papery side of the fusible web facing up. Trace the template onto the fusible web using a pencil.

2 Cut out the shape, leaving a ¼" (6mm) allowance around the entire edge.

3 Place the fusible web, with the fusible (nonpapery) side down, onto the wrong side of the appliqué fabric. Fuse the web to the fabric with an iron, following the manufacturer's instructions.

4 Cut along the pencil markings on the paper backing. Remove the paper backing.

5 Place the appliqué with the right side of the fabric facing up in the desired spot on the right side of the background fabric and fuse, following the manufacturer's instructions. Pin the appliqué securely to prevent any further movement; despite being fused down, it may shift slightly while warm.

6 Sew around the perimeter of the appliqué with a zigzag stitch or satin stitch. For shorter outlines use a shorter-length stitch, and for larger pieces use a longer stitch. Bury the loose threads under the stitches on the wrong side by hand.

MAKING BIAS TAPE You can buy bias tape (also called bias trim) or make your own. With a few easy, calculated steps, you will have unlimited options compared to what's available in stores. In addition to basic sewing supplies, you'll need a bias tape maker, which makes folding bias tape a whole lot easier. I prefer using a rotary cutter and self-healing mat, but scissors will do, too.

1 Start with approximately 1 yard (0.9m) of fabric, and lay it right side up. (One yard [0.9m] of fabric makes about 18 yards [16.5m] of ½" [13mm] double-fold bias tape. That's a whole lot of bias tape!) Fold one corner of the fabric so that the right sides are together and the selvage edges are lined up. Press the folded edge,

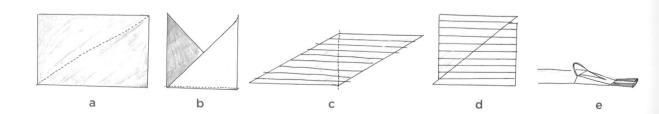

a   b   c   d   e

unfold the fabric, and cut down the line. I prefer using a rotary cutter because it gives a nice, precise line (a).

2 After the pieces are cut, place them right sides together, matching up the shorter straight edges; the points create a V. Pin and sew together (b). Lay the fabric out and press the seam open.

3 Using a long straightedge, draw the lines for the overall width of the bias trim (c).

4 Fold over and match the rows, offsetting them by one row. Carefully cut the lines to make long strips (d).

5 Feed the fabric strips into the bias tape maker and iron (e). You now have custom bias tape!

HEMMING A hem gives weight to the fabric to ensure that it drapes correctly. I am a big fan of the double hem and use it most often in this book. Hems can also be hand-sewn using a slip stitch (page 19).

1 Use tailor's chalk to mark a line of small dashes where you want the first fold to be from the edge, fold the fabric edge to that mark, and press that fold in place.

2 Turn that fold over again in the exact same width, press, and pin in place. Edge stitch around the entire perimeter of the hem.

RIPPING OUT STITCHES A seam ripper is a magical tool when you make a mistake. Starting at one end of the unwanted seam, break a line of stitches every couple inches through the entire seam. When you are done, the back thread will pull out easily. Make sure to remove all the loose threads, which could otherwise get tangled in your machine when you redo the seam.

quilting techniques

The idea of quilting can be daunting at first, but the basic projects in this book will help you conquer your fear of quilting, so much so, you'll be ready (and wanting) to try more.

PREPPING A QUILT I highly recommend the following supplies for any quilting project: a rotary cutter and self-healing mat, quilting ruler (this is great to have for all sewing purposes), and glass-head pins. In addition, every quilting project requires batting and quilting thread (page 14). The following steps explain the basic technique to assemble and finish a quilt:

1 Cut out the three layers and stack them as follows: back (right side down), batting, and top (right side up).

2 Baste the layers together by hand with long stitches, then hand- or machine-sew the pieces together, following your desired quilting technique (page 24).

3 Finish the edges with bias tape, or make the backing fabric slightly larger to fold toward the top and stitch it in place.

4 Adjust the machine to the desired stitch length (usually 2.5mm) and straight-stitch in the seam.

- -

snip! snip!

Always snip the excess thread as you work. I recommend using a small pair of embroidery scissors.

- -

STITCH IN THE DITCH This quilting technique involves sewing a row of stitches in the seam that lies between two different fabric blocks. The thread will be hidden in the seams but visible on the back, so choose your thread color accordingly.

1 If not instructed in your pattern, decide which seam lines you are going to stitch.

2 Securely pin or baste the layers of fabric and batting to prevent any movement. Start pinning in the center and move outward.

FREE-MOTION QUILTING This technique gives you complete reign over the direction and length you want in a stitch. It definitely takes practice, but once you have mastered it, the possibilities are endless. You'll need a free-motion quilting foot plus, if you aren't using this technique on a quilt, an embroidery hoop to keep the fabric taut. Free-motion quilting involves lowering the machine's feed dogs and releasing the pressure on the pressure foot, so that *you* (not the machine) have complete control of the direction and length of the stitches. I love this technique so much because it allows me to "draw" on fabric with my sewing machine.

note
The slower you move the fabric, the closer the stitches will be. The faster you move the fabric around, the longer the stitches.

1 Replace the regular sewing foot with the free-motion foot, and lower the feed dogs.

2 Attach the fabric you want to draw on onto an embroidery hoop. Choose an

Free-motion quilting allows you to create quirky embroidered embellishments.

appropriate-size hoop for the portion you want to free-motion quilt.

3 Raise the presser foot and place the embroidery hoop under it. Depending on what you are sewing, it may be beneficial to put some type of interfacing on the back of the fabric to prevent the fabric from puckering.

4 Lower the presser foot and choose the desired stitch. I typically use a short straight stitch, but remember that you have control over the length of the stitches based on how you move the embroidery hoop. If stitching a quilt, begin in the center and move outward. Hold the quilt or the edge of the embroidery hoop and move it around to draw on the fabric with the machine. If you aren't confident with drawing freehand (it will take a couple rounds of practice to get used to this technique), use a washable fabric marker to draw on the fabric as a guide.

finish it off!

You have a few options when you are finishing seams. If you look at the inside of a store-bought garment, you will notice seams that have a lot of thread tightly woven around the raw edges. This was done with a serger, which is yet another sewing tool. But let's keep things simple here! Although I have a serger, I don't really use it often, and I think my regular machine does a fine job of sewing up the seams using these tools and techniques.

PINKING SHEARS This is by far the easiest method, though it isn't always the neatest way to go about finishing a seam. With pinking shears, trim along the seam line,

being careful not to clip the seam. This zigzag cut helps prevent the threads of the garment from unraveling.

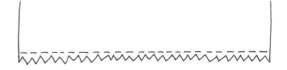

ZIGZAG STITCH Try this on a test fabric first because, depending on the type of fabric, the stitch length and width might need to be adjusted so the seam will lie nicely without too much bulk. Once you have the right stitch figured out, zigzag down the entire length of the seam (page 18). The threads will weave themselves tightly around the edges, giving the garment a serger-like finish.

FRENCH SEAMS This seam is typically done for thin and delicate fabrics that fray easily, but it is also a great way to finish off edges if you don't have access to a serger. The raw edges are hidden inside, which in turn creates a clean seam.

1 Place the wrong sides together with the raw edges aligned. Straight stitch ¼" (6mm) from the cut edges.

2 Press the joined edges flat and press the seam open.

3 Refold the seam allowance with the right sides of the fabric together. To finish the French seam, stitch slightly less than ¼″ (6mm) from the fold, enclosing the raw edges and the first seam.

adding closures

I used to be intimidated by the thought of sewing a buttonhole or adding a zipper, but as I practiced, I have become much more confident with closures.

BUTTONHOLES Modern sewing machines are fancy and almost always come with an automatic buttonhole foot. If you don't have one, get one! It is well worth the investment. Every machine will vary slightly, but basically you will place the button into the top of the foot, attach the buttonhole foot to the presser foot leg, and adjust the machine to its proper settings for buttonholes. I typically leave the stitch length at 3 stitches per inch (spi) and make sure that the stitch width is close to 0 spi, which creates stitches that are very close together and prevents fraying. Using the button and a water-soluble pen, mark where you want the button to be on the right side of the fabric. Using the mark as a guide, allow the machine to sew the buttonhole. Cut the buttonhole open with a seam ripper, being careful not to cut any

doubled thread

Typically, I like to use two strands of thread when doing any hand-work. The extra reinforcement just makes me feel better.

of the threads of the sewn buttonhole. Snip any loose threads.

BUTTONS There are two types of buttons: sew-through buttons and shank buttons.

SEW-THROUGH BUTTONS

1 With a knotted strand of thread, insert the needle and thread through one of the holes from the wrong side of the fabric.

2 Place a toothpick on top of the button, and bring the needle and thread over the toothpick and down through the opposite hole. Repeat this motion a few times (a).

3 Remove the toothpick and pull the button up on the excess thread. Wind the thread around the loose thread under the button to create a shank (b).

4 Tie the threads on the back side of the fabric with a finishing knot and snip the excess thread (c).

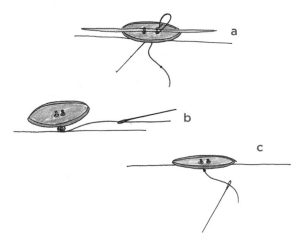

SHANK BUTTONS

1 With a knotted thread, make a small stitch on the fabric where the center of the button will be.

2 Insert the needle and thread through the hole on the shank button and pull it through.

3 Slightly tilt the button upward and bring the needle and thread through the shank a couple of times.

4 Wind the thread lightly around the thread shank and create a loop of thread on one side of the threads and bring the needle through the loop. Pull the threads tight. Bring the needle and thread back through the back side of the fabric and end with a finishing knot. Snip off the excess thread.

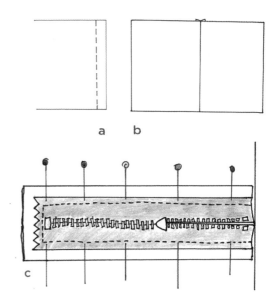

ZIPPERS

1 Mark the zipper's placement on the project. With the right sides together, baste the zipper placket together (a).

2 Press the seam open (b) and finish the seam edges to prevent unraveling with a zigzag stitch or another finishing technique (page 25).

3 Center the zipper teeth, right side up, under the basted seam allowance. Pull the zipper tab down to help reduce bulk at the top of the zipper. Pin the zipper tape to the seam allowances (c).

4 On the right side of the fabric, beginning at the seam, topstitch across the zipper base, pivoting at the corner and continuing to the top edge of the zipper.

5 Move the needle position and stitch from the seam line at the zipper base to the upper edge along the opposite side.

6 Snip off the threads on the wrong side of the fabric and remove the basting stitches with a seam ripper.

zipper too long?

Mark the length of the zipper with a fabric marker. Using a zigzag stitch set to the widest stitch and a length of 0 spi, sew several stitches across the marked spot. This will act as a stopper for the zipper. Cut off the remainder of the zipper that is no longer needed.

book it

Fabrics A to Z (STC Craft, 2012) by Dana Willard is a must for any sewer. It provides full descriptions of various fabrics, what they are best used for, and what types of needles to use. Always keep a handy reference book like this one nearby when you sew.

sewing vocabulary

These are a few terms and phrases that you will see throughout the book.

APPLIQUÉ: Sewing a smaller fabric shape on a larger piece of background fabric.

BASTING: Temporarily binding layers of fabric with long, removable stitches.

BATTING: The material used as stuffing between the quilt top and quilt backing.

BIAS: The direction that runs at a 45-degree angle to the grain of fabric.

BINDING: A narrow strip of fabric that is cut on the bias. This is also called bias tape.

EDGE STITCH: Sewing a straight stitch close to the edge of your fabric.

GRAIN: The direction in which threads run through a piece of fabric.

INTERFACING: A special fabric added to the wrong side of fabric to give it more body or structure.

LINING: The separate inner layer of fabric, such as the inside fabric of a bag or pouch.

MITER: A joint that forms a corner.

NOTIONS: Sewing tools or accessories that are listed before the project instructions.

PRESS: Iron your seams as you go to keep them neat.

RAW EDGE: The cut edge of a fabric before it is finished.

RIGHT SIDE: The side of the fabric or project that is to be seen.

SEAM: A line where two pieces of fabric are sewn together.

SEAM ALLOWANCE: The distance between the line of stitching and the raw edge of the fabric.

SELVAGE: The edges of fabric that typically include the designer and care information.

SLIP STITCH: A hand-sewing technique to close openings in pillows and softies.

STITCH IN THE DITCH: Stitching a straight stitch in between a seam, used in quilting.

TOPSTITCH: A straight stitch created on top of a seam.

TURN: Flip the fabric inside out or vice versa using a point turner (or chopstick).

WRONG SIDE: The underside of the fabric.

kid-friendly sewing

You've mastered the basics of sewing; now how can you teach your kids? Sewing is an easy concept for kids to understand, because it just requires following lines and shapes. It teaches them to follow directions, recognize a number sequence, and see a picture come to life by creating simple lines.

I started allowing my girls to sew with a dull hand needle and embroidery hoop around the age of four. They didn't make anything in particular, but practiced the up-and-down motion of the needle through the fabric. It did turn out to be a tangled mess, but it was a fun hand-eye coordination project to do together, even if they weren't perfectly coordinated yet. If you feel adventurous (and think they're ready), teach them how to sew a straight line on the sewing machine. Remember always to supervise and reinforce the proper safety tips (at right). If they're not quite ready for needles and a sewing machine, you'll still find plenty of opportunities to get them involved. For example, they can choose the fabrics for each continent in the Travel the World Quilt (page 99), or weave the fabric in the Colorful Plaid A-frame Tent (page 143). Here are a few safety tips, guidelines, and projects to teach kids how to get comfortable with sewing.

sewing safety tips

1 Watch the fingers. A machine needle can move fast, so always keep fingers far away from the needle to protect them. Remember, the feed dogs guide the fabric through, so your fingers don't need to be near the needle when it is in operation. Let the needle and the feed dogs do their jobs.

2 When using a seam ripper, make sure to cut away from the body, with the sharp end pointed away from you.

3 Unplug the machine when not in use. This helps prevent curious little ones from accidentally turning it on and possibly getting hurt. A machine sounds fun and has moving parts that will make kids curious, but it isn't a toy and should never be left unattended around babies and children.

4 Pay attention when cutting fabric or paper. Before you start cutting with scissors or a rotary cutter, make sure that your fingers are not in the path of the blade.

5 Use a thimble. It protects the middle finger when sewing by hand.

age-appropriate sewing tasks

While your child may not yet be able to do some sewing, he or she can still get involved in the process. Here's a little set of guidelines to get them involved in the projects based on their age or skill level. All the projects in this book are about sewing and playing together, so try these tips to make sure everyone can contribute.

AGES TWO TO THREE
- Scribble on fabric with fabric markers or paint.
- Choose colorful fabrics. They might not necessarily match, but the project will be special because they picked it!
- With a parent's guidance, weave fabric strips, such as in the Colorful Plaid A-frame Tent (page 143).

AGES FOUR TO SIX
- Stuff softies or puppets with polyester fiberfill.
- Draw unique designs to use for appliqués.
- Hand pins carefully to a parent who is pinning fabric.
- Make pom-poms (page 33) or tassels for decorative trim.
- Braid fabric strips together, as in the Ship-Shapes Fabric Necklace (page 39).

AGES SEVEN TO TEN
- Cut out paper templates and fabric.
- Pin fabrics.
- Do simple hand-sewing or embroidery with an embroidery hoop.
- With a parent's guidance, learn basic stitches, such as a simple straight stitch, on a sewing machine.
- Pick out coordinating fabrics using a color wheel.
- Pull elastic through a casing, such as in The Full & Fun Skirt (page 49) or Running in the Sun Shorts (page 53).

perfectly pom pincushion

With all this sewing talk, I'm sure that you can't wait to get started. Here's a quick project to practice a straight stitch. When you are done, you will have a cute little pincushion to aid you in the rest of your projects. It involves some simple machine sewing, so if you think your child is ready to try it, guide him or her through the steps. Otherwise, children can get involved by learning how to make pom-poms (page 33).

skill level

Sew Quick ⓢ

materials

Basic sewing supplies (page 12)

Two 5½" x 5½" (14cm x 14cm) fabric squares

Polyester fiberfill

1½" x 3" (3.8cm x 7.5cm) piece of cardboard

7 yards (6.4m) plus 12" (30.5cm) of yarn

seam allowance

½" (13mm)

finished measurements

Approximately 5" x 5" (12.5cm x 12.5cm)

1 Place the 5½" x 5½" (14cm x 14cm) fabric squares with their right sides together and pin.

2 Stitch the entire perimeter, leaving a 2" (5cm) opening in one side for turning. Clip the corners, turn, and press the fabric.

3 Stuff with polyester fiberfill until the square is somewhat firm, and slip stitch the opening closed.

4 Using the cardboard and the length of yarn, make a pom-pom (page 33). Fluff the pom-pom and trim if necessary to even out the shape.

5 Center and hand-sew the pom-pom on the pincushion, stitching through the center back of the cushion, and then through the pom-pom to the front center. Bring the needle and thread through the back again. Tie and knot the thread and bury the tails to fasten the pom-pom tightly.

how to make a pom-pom

Get your child involved in making the pom-pom, and he or she will want to make pom-poms all afternoon, in every color of the rainbow.

Cut a piece of cardboard about the width you want the pom-pom to be, and at least 10" (25.5cm) long. Cut a slit across the middle to the center (a). Insert a 12" (30.5cm) strand of yarn and let it hang evenly on both sides of the slit. Wrap yarn around the cardboard until you reach the desired thickness (b). Using the 12" (30.5cm) strand, tie a secure knot around the wrapped yarn (c). Make sure to pull it tight before knotting. Slide the pom-pom off the cardboard. Cut through all the loops (d). And just like that, you have a pom-pom (e)! The pom-pom may require shaping, so trim around it as needed.

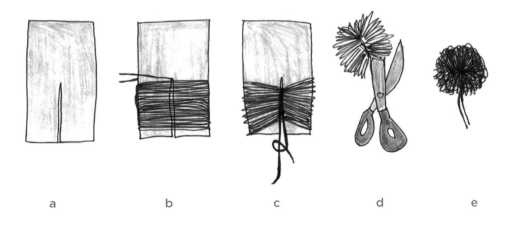

a   b   c   d   e

homemade sewing cards

Teach the basic stitches of hand-sewing using sewing cards. It's another fun way for children to play connect-the-dots and practice the in-and-out motion of sewing using their illustrations.

materials for one card

Drawing supplies (pencils, markers, crayons, etc.)

5½" x 8½" (14 cm x 21.5cm) piece of card stock

Hole punch or small screwdriver

24" (61cm) piece of yarn or string

Plastic sewing needle

note

To take the project a step further for older children, print the sewing-card illustrations onto iron-on transfer paper. (Take note to print the image mirrored, otherwise the numbers will come out flipped.) Iron the image onto a light-colored fabric, place the fabric in an embroidery hoop, and practice sewing by connecting the dots with an embroidery needle and embroidery floss.

1 Draw and color a picture on the card stock. Pierce holes along the shape of the picture about ½" (13mm) apart with a hole punch or a small screwdriver. I find that, depending on how close the image gets to the edge, it's sometimes easier to pierce holes using a small screwdriver.

2 Thread the yarn or string through the plastic sewing needle.

3 Have your child sew around the picture with the yarn and plastic needle. Push the needle up from the wrong side of the card and down through the right side until the picture is complete. To reinforce counting, number each hole in consecutive order and say the numbers out loud as the dots are connected.

more practice!

You can find premade sewing cards at a local craft shop, or an even greater variety online. I especially love scouting for vintage sewing cards.

let's get dressed!

If you peeked into our home in the mornings, you would hear chaos as we get our four girls ready to go out. Some may call our house full of happy noises, and others may say it sounds like a whole lot of stress. Either way, this is a part of family life that I cherish.

Despite our own preferences about what we'd like our children to wear, kids discover their personality through their own choices. And we get to know more about them by watching them decide. One of my daughters has grown through a layer-all-you-can phase, and for a while another always insisted on tucking her dresses into her pants. Always. No matter what silly phases they go through, you'll both look back on these times and giggle.

The projects in this chapter will give them (and you) an opportunity to become mini fashion designers with simple-to-sew garments and outrageously fun accessories. With a few special tools, kids can even draw somewhere they normally aren't allowed to: on their clothes! Have fun with your children deciding on a design to add to a dress, how to personalize a pair of shorts, or what secret treasures to make for their pockets.

Getting a family ready in the morning can be a hassle, but it can also be a creative, memorable experience. Enjoy the morning chaos.

ship-shapes
fabric necklace

This fabric necklace just screams fun and adds pizzazz to any outfit. It's also a great way to teach young children about shapes. After they have finished drawing, the grown-up or an older child can stitch the pieces together.

skill level
Sew Quick ⏺

materials
Basic sewing supplies (page 12)

Fabric markers or fabric paint and paintbrushes

¼ yard (23cm) of light-colored fabric for the front

¼ yard (23cm) of coordinating fabric for the back

Polyester fiberfill

Three 1" x 13" (2.5cm x 33cm) strips of fabric

Embroidery floss

seam allowance
¼" (6mm)

notes
- Use colorful fabric choices for the braided part of the necklace.
- Instead of fabric markers, use fabric paint (page 15), or cut the shapes out of fun patterned fabrics.
- For an ultra-fabulous necklace, make the various shapes different sizes or even omit the braided string and make the necklace entirely out of shapes sewn together.

continues

1 Using fabric markers, draw and color 5 circles and 5 triangles onto t he light-colored fabric. (You can make 2 necklaces with 10 shapes.) Circles should be at least 2" (5cm) in diameter, and triangles about 2½" (6.5cm) high. Space the shapes about 1" (2.5cm) apart to allow room for cutting.

read it together!

The Greedy Triangle
by Marilyn Burns

The Shape of Me and Other Stuff
by Dr. Seuss

My Very First Book of Shapes
by Eric Carle

Sir Cumference and the First Round Table
by Cindy Neuschwander

2 Place the fabric with hand-drawn shapes on top of the backing fabric with wrong sides together. Line up the edges of the fabrics. Follow the edges of the shapes and cut an extra ¼" (6mm) around each (a).

3 With the two coordinating pieces of fabric wrong sides together (the drawn shape and backing fabric), sew around the shape, ¼" (6mm) from the edge, but leave a 1" (2.5cm) opening for filling.

4 Lightly fill each piece to the desired thickness (b), and sew the shape closed (c).

5 To create the braided fabric string, cut three 1" x 13" (2.5cm x 33cm) strips of fabric for each necklace. Practice braiding with your child, then sew each end with a straight stitch and backstitch to secure. Set aside the braids.

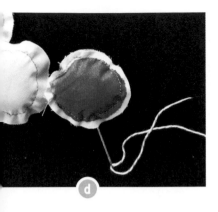

teaching moments

- Identify the various types of triangles: isosceles, equilateral, acute, obtuse, scalene, and right angle.

- *Circumference* is the distance around a circle, *radius* is the distance from the center of the circle to the edge, and *diameter* is the measurement across the circle.

6 With the hand-sewing needle and embroidery floss, string through the seam of each fabric shape and connect each piece together, as if you were stringing beads together (d). Each necklace uses 5 fabric shapes. Mix the triangle and circular shapes together, or keep them in separate necklaces as pictured. Once each piece is strung together, hand-sew one end to the braided strap, then repeat with the remaining end of the fabric shapes and the remaining braided strap.

7 To create an entire necklace with the shapes, eliminate the braided straps and use fabric shapes around the entire length of the necklace and knot the ends of the twine or floss together.

sweetly sketch & tie reversible frock

Drawing on our clothes started when my oldest daughter wanted to make one of her little sisters a birthday dress. She bugged me for days to help her make a dress as a gift. She picked the fabric, but I did most of the sewing. To add more of herself into it (this was her gift idea, after all), she drew on another scrap of fabric, which we appliquéd onto the dress. An instant one-of-a-kind present from one sister to another!

skill level
Make in an Afternoon ⊙ ⊙

materials
Basic sewing supplies (page 12)

Sweetly Sketch & Tie Reversible Frock template (page 167)

Fabric for outer dress:
Size 12–24 months: 1¼ yards (1.1m)
Size 4–6: 1½ yards (1.4m)
Size 8–10: 1⅞ yards (1.8m)

Contrasting fabric for reversible dress:
Size 12–24 months: 1¼ yards (1.1m)
Size 4–6: 1½ yards (1.4m)
Size 8–10: 1⅞ yards (1.8m)

Fabric markers or fabric paint and paintbrushes

Scrap cardboard or stack of scrap papers

Embroidery hoop

Embroidery floss

Buttons (optional)

seam allowance
½" (13mm) except where otherwise noted

continues

1 Cut out all the pattern pieces. There are 5 total: outer dress front, outer dress back, reversible dress front, reversible dress back, and pocket (page 58). Feel free to omit the pocket or add another to hold more treasures.

2 With the fabric markers or paint, have your child sketch pictures in a designated spot on the outer front of the dress—or let her go to town all over the dress (a). Be sure the drawings stay at least 1" (2.5cm) in from the side edges and 3" (7.5cm) up from the bottom edge; otherwise, the side seams and bottom hem will hide the drawings. Allow the drawings to dry completely, then iron the drawn images to heat-set them.

note
Place a scrap board or a stack of papers under the areas that will be drawn on, as sometimes the color will bleed through.

3 Place the area to be embroidered in an embroidery hoop, and with a needle and embroidery floss, embroider portions of the design (b) with backstitch (page 20).

read it together!

Zoe Gets Ready
by Bethanie Murguia

Ella Sarah Gets Dressed
by Margaret
Chodos-Irvine

Get Dressed!
by Seymour Chwast

*The Hueys in
The New Sweater*
by Oliver Jeffers

A New Coat for Anna
by Harriet Ziefert

The Hundred Dresses
by Eleanor Estes

I Had a Favorite Dress
by Boni Ashburn

Different Like Coco
by Elizabeth Matthews

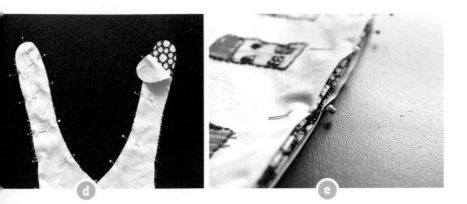

Once the design is embroidered, press the dress front again.

4 Place the pocket on the reversible dress front, pin in place, and edge stitch around the 3 sides, leaving the top open. Embellish with a button (c).

5 Pin the outer dress front and outer dress back right sides together and sew down the entire length of both sides. Press the seams open.

6 Pin the reversible dress front and reversible dress back right sides together and sew down the entire length of both sides. Press the seams open.

7 Place the reversible dress inside the outer dress with their right sides together, carefully lining up the neckline and straps, and pin them in place (d). With a ¼" (6mm) seam allowance, sew around the straps, arms, and neckline.

Clip around all the curves, turn right side out, and press.

8 Make sure the length is right for your child; feel free to cut off more of the length if you desire something a bit shorter. Fold in the outer dress and reversible dress hemline ½" (13mm) around the entire length, press, and pin in place (e). Topstitch ¼" (6mm) from the folded edge to finish the hem. Press the entire dress.

notes
- Since the dress is reversible, it is best to use a lightweight cotton fabric to prevent making the dress too heavy.
- The dress can easily be changed into a shirt by shortening the length.
- If Mom gets a strong urge to make one for herself, just keep playing with a copier and enlarge this simple pattern until it's the perfect grown-up size!

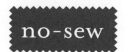

bobby's bow ties

These wacky and fun bow ties are sure to make your little lad's outfit a wee bit dapper. Colorful bows are also an easy—and adorable—way to smarten up a girl's outfit.

materials

3" x 9" (7.5cm x 23cm) piece of wool or acrylic felt

Fabric glue

60" (152.5cm) strand of contrasting colored yarn

Plastic lacing needle

finished measurements

3" x 4" (7.5cm x 10cm)

notes

• Only children age three and older should wear this project around the neck as a bow tie.

• There are so many ways to wear bows: tie one to a piece of ribbon for a bracelet, glue to a hair barrette, or pin on the lapel of a little jacket.

1 Overlap the short ends of the felt fabric ½" (13mm) and add a touch of glue along the edge to secure the ends in place (a).

2 Fold the piece in half lengthwise and wrap a 36" (91cm) strand of yarn around the center. Tightly tie the strand around the center to get the bow tie shape (b). Once most of the strand has been wound around the center, securely knot it at the back.

3 With the remaining 24" (61cm) strand of yarn, thread it on the plastic lacing needle, insert and pull it through the yarn on the back of the bow tie, and knot it securely (c).

the full & fun skirt

Yes, this skirt really is full and fun!
Full skirts are great for twirling,
gathering treasures, and playing
princess. Plus, a full skirt allows
plenty of surface area for young
textile designers to add lots of
patterns with fabric paint. Adding
their own designs is always my
children's most favorite part of a
project like this one.

skill level
Sew Quick 😊

materials
Basic sewing supplies (page 12)

1 yard (0.9m) of fabric
(or more, depending on
measurements in step 1)

Fabric paint and paintbrushes

¾"- (2cm-) wide elastic
(length will depend on
measurements in step 6)

Safety pin

seam allowance
½" (13mm)

notes
- Choose a paint that contrasts with the fabric
  color for a bolder choice or paint a design
  on patterned fabric to give the skirt an extra
  dimension.
- To avoid a muddy mess, use one color of
  paint at a time and allow it to dry completely
  before layering another color.
- Have fun choosing the fabrics and creating
  patterns on it together.

dress-up fun

Make a game out of
getting dressed. Set a
timer and make getting
dressed a race. Or
pick out an outfit that
showcases every color of the rainbow.

continues

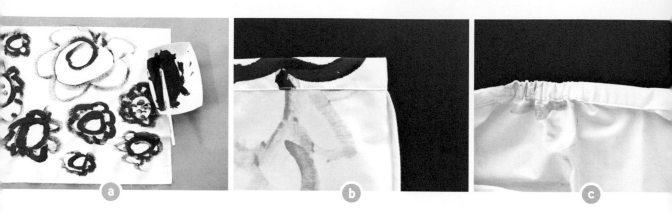

1 Measure your child's waist circumference (for the width of the skirt). Measure for the desired length and add 3" (7.5cm). Cut out 2 rectangular fabric pieces to those measurements.

note
Doubling the waist size creates a really full skirt; for less volume, cut 2 narrower rectangles.

2 Paint shapes and designs all over both skirt pieces. Let the paint dry completely and iron to heat-set it (a).

3 Sew one side seam together with a French seam (page 25) and press the seam flat.

4 Sew the other side seam with a French seam and press the seam flat.

5 To make the waistband casing, turn down the top edge ½" (13mm), press; turn down another 1" (2.5cm), press, and pin. Edge stitch close to the folded edge, leaving a 2" (5cm) opening to weave the elastic through (b).

6 Cut the elastic by measuring around your child's waist and subtracting 3"–5" (7.5cm–12.5cm), or whatever will be most comfortable for your child (one of my daughters doesn't like elastic that's too tight), then attach a safety pin to one end of the elastic and carefully push it through the casing. Once completely through, overlap the elastic ends ½" (13mm) and sew them together with a straight stitch. Backstitch to reinforce. Stitch the remaining opening closed (c).

7 Allowing for a 1" (2.5cm) hem, make sure the skirt length is right for your child; trim if necessary. Turn up the hem ½" (13mm) and press. Turn up another ½" (13mm), press, and pin in place. Topstitch ½" (13mm) from the folded edge to finish off the hem.

barrette baubles

My kids lose hair clips all the time, so these colorful adornments are quick and simple enough to make over and over again! Make a few of them to wrap up in cute packaging for a little gift.

materials

Glue gun and glue sticks

French barrette,
    1½"–2" (3.8cm–5cm) long
    (choose an appropriate
    size for your child)

Trinkets for embellishing clips:
    pom-poms, plastic jewels,
    or buttons

Glue trinkets onto the top of the barrettes. Mix up the colors and designs. Make them as colorful as possible!

running in the sun shorts

The sun is shining, and all you want to do is be outside. Personalized with an embroidered monogram and optional Secret Treasure Toy (page 58), these shorts are just right for this weather! In this project, you'll practice creating an elasticized waistband and two types of pockets.

skill level
Make in an Afternoon ⊙ ⊙

materials

Basic sewing supplies (page 12)

Running in the Sun Shorts template (page 168)

Fabric
> **Size 12–24 months:** ⅔ yard (61cm)
> **Size 4–6:** ⅞ yard (0.8m)
> **Size 8–10:** 1 yard (0.9m)

Embroidery floss for a monogram (optional)

Pockets & Secret Treasure Toys (page 57; optional)

¾"- (2cm-) wide elastic (measure the exact length in step 10)

Safety pin

seam allowance
½" (13mm)

notes
- Customize by embroidering the pockets or adding ribbon or trim to the hem of the shorts.
- These can be made into longer pants.

continues

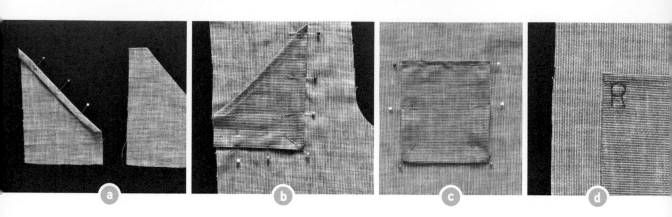

1 Cut out all pattern pieces: 2 shorts front, 2 shorts back, and 2 front pockets plus (optional) 2 back pockets.

2 Fold down the top slanted edge of the front pocket pieces ¼" (6mm), press, and fold down another ¼" (6mm). Press again, pin, and topstitch in place (a). Fold the inner pocket edges and pocket bottoms ¼" (6mm) under and press. Leave the outer side pocket edges unfolded; they will be sewn into the seam allowance.

3 With right side facing up, place the front pockets 2½" (6.5cm) down from the top of the shorts fronts, lining up the side edges with the raw edges of the side of the front short pieces. Pin the sides and bottom in place (b). Edge stitch the inner side pocket and the bottom of the pocket in place. Don't sew the side that is lined up with the raw edges just yet.

4 If desired, cut out the pocket fabric pieces, draw a monogram with an air-fading marker on the upper corner of a back pocket piece, and embroider it with embroidery floss and a backstitch (page 20). Make back pockets (page 58), place them on the back of the shorts about 3"–3½" (7.5–9cm) from the top and about 1½"–2" (3.8–5cm) from the side, pin in place (c), and sew around three sides, leaving the top of the pocket open (d).

5 With right sides together, match the front center seams, and pin in place (e). Sew the front center seams together. Repeat for the back center seams. Zigzag-stitch the center seams to finish the edges (page 25).

6 Match the front and back short pieces with right sides together, lining up the side edges, and pin in place. If including

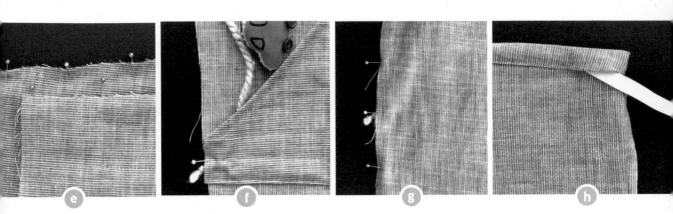

a Secret Treasure Toy (page 58), place it inside the pocket and extend the open end of the yarn ½" (13mm) off the side of the outer pocket (f). Sew down the entire length of the side of the shorts (g). Press the seam open. Repeat for the other side. Zigzag-stitch the entire length of the side seams to finish the edges and reinforce them (or sew them with a French seam using a ¼" [6mm] seam allowance).

7 Open the front and back short pieces, right sides still together. Pin the inner leg seams together, and sew from the bottom of one short leg to the other. Zigzag-stitch the entire length of the side seams to finish the edges and reinforce them.

8 Fold up the bottom hem of each leg ½" (13mm), press, fold up another ½" (13mm), press, and pin in place. Topstitch around close to the folded edge to finish the hem. Repeat for the remaining short leg.

9 To make the waistband casing, turn down the top edge ½" (13mm), press; turn down another 1" (2.5cm), press, and pin. Edge stitch close to the folded edge, leaving a 2" (5cm) opening to slide the elastic through.

10 Measure around your child's waist and subtract 5" (12.5cm), or whatever is comfortable for your child. Cut a length of elastic to this measurement. Attach a safety pin to one end of the elastic and carefully slide it through the casing (h). Overlap the elastic ends by ½" (13mm) and sew them together with a straight stitch. Backstitch to reinforce. Topstitch the remaining opening closed.

pockets & secret treasure toys

If an outfit needs more oomph, just try adding a pocket in a coordinating (or not-so-coordinating) fabric. Easy-to-sew pockets add visual interest to a garment, and the hidden toys make them even more interesting for the child wearing them.

skill level
Sew Quick ⊕

materials
Basic sewing supplies (page 12)

Pockets & Secret Treasure Toys template (page 169)

Fabric for the pockets (I used a 5" x 6" [12.5cm x 15cm] piece for these pockets, but they can be any size)

3" x 3" (7.5cm x 7.5cm) scraps of wool felt or cotton fabric for the toys

Fabric markers or fabric paint and paintbrushes

10"–12" (25.5–30.5cm) of yarn or ribbon (optional)

Polyester fiberfill

Button (optional)

seam allowance
¼" (6mm)

finished measurements
Each toy is 2" x 3" (5cm x 7.5cm)

continues

pocket

1 Draw your desired pocket size. Using a seam gauge, add an additional 1" (2.5cm) to the top and ¼" (6mm) to each of the remaining 3 sides (a).

2 Fold down the top edge ½" (13mm), press, fold down another ½" (13mm), press, pin in place, and topstitch (b).

3 Fold the remaining 3 sides in ¼" (6mm) and press.

4 Place the pocket on the desired spot on the garment, right side facing up, pin the folded sides in place, and edge stitch around the 3 sides (c).

5 To add a decorative button to the pocket, center it ½" (13mm) from the top of the pocket and hand-sew in place.

secret treasure toy

1 Use the template or your own shape and cut out the small fabric pieces and coordinating backing fabric.

2 Draw designs and shapes on the little fabric pieces (d). This is a good place for younger children to help out, if they can't sew yet. Add any additional wool felt embellishments if desired.

3 Place the coordinating fabric pieces with their right sides together (the drawn fabric piece and its coordinating back). Sew around the edges, leaving a 1" (2.5cm) opening for turning. If attaching yarn or ribbon, cut it to the desired length extending from the pocket. Sandwich the string between the right sides of the fabric, with one end of the string extended ½" (13mm) off the raw edge of the fabric (e). Clip the curves, turn right side out, and press (f).

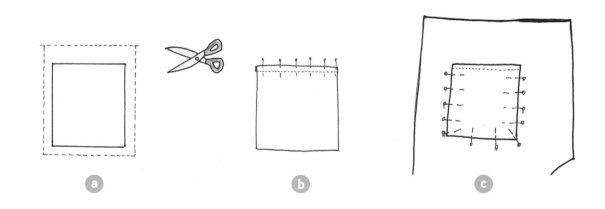

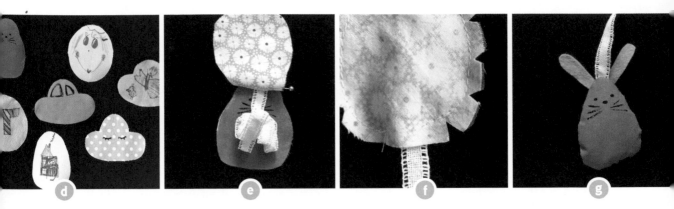

4 Stuff with polyester fiberfill to the desired thickness and slip stitch the opening closed (g).

5 If the pocket treasure has a yarn or ribbon to attach to a pocket, place the unattached string end extended ½" (13mm) off the side of the pocket. Continue to edge stitch the sides of the pocket, attaching it to the garment, and attaching the string in the process. Cut the remaining ½" (13mm) of the string from the side. If the pocket has a button on the front, just tie one end of the string to the back of the button.

note
Stitch or glue a pin to the back and the pocket toys become fun brooches that can be pinned on dresses, shirts, backpacks, and even other toys!

way cool wristlets

Handmade swag, just the way you want it. These oven-baked accessories for girls or boys are like a party on your arm!

materials

Oven-bake modeling clay

Little roller for the clay

1½" (3.8cm) circle cut from card stock

Plastic knife

Hand-sewing needle

Permanent markers or acrylic paint and paintbrushes

Two 6" (15cm) pieces of elastic cording (you may need more depending on what's comfortable for your child's wrist)

note
Only children age three and older should wear this project around the wrist.

1 Take a pinch of modeling clay and roll it out flat to ¼" (6mm) thickness. Place the card-stock circle on top of the flattened clay and use it as a template to cut a circle from the clay with a plastic knife.

2 With a hand-sewing needle, poke two holes on opposite sides of the clay circle about ⅛" (3mm) in from the edge (a). Follow manufacturer's instructions for baking the clay.

3 Let your child paint or draw fun designs on the baked and cooled circle face. It might be a superhero bracelet, or show off some pretty flowers; it could be a magic teleporter or maybe a hidden microphone wristlet. Allow his or her imagination to guide what the wristlet will be.

4 Insert each strand of cording into one hole, pass it under the clay circle. Gather the ends at the back of the wristlet, and securely knot them to the appropriate size (b).

super-happy slippers

Imagine your child frolicking about the house with drawings on her feet and a smile on her face. These slippers are a simple project to help you learn free-motion quilting, too! Make another pair of these artsy slippers for yourself or to give as a gift.

skill level
Make in an Afternoon ⊕ ⊕

materials
Basic sewing supplies (page 12)

Paper and pencil for tracing the foot

Ruler

¼ yard (23cm) of fabric
(or sew pieces of fabric together to make the slippers extra colorful)

¼ yard (23cm) of cotton batting

¼ yard (23cm) of nonskid fabric
(this allows for plenty of leftover fabric to make another pair)

¼ yard (23cm) of thick polyester batting

Fabric markers or fabric paint and paintbrushes

Free-motion quilting foot with quilting thread or embroidery floss

seam allowance
½" (13mm)

note
These slippers can be made in all sorts of fun ways! Use patterned fabric, embroider your child's name, or leave them plain.

continues

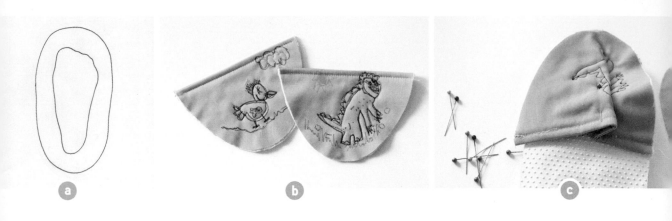

a

b

c

1 Trace your child's foot. With a seam gauge, add 1" (2.5cm) around the perimeter of the traced foot. Using that shape as a guide, create a long oval shape for the slipper sole template (a).

2 Lay out the slipper sole template on another sheet of paper and create a template for the slipper top. Measure 5" (12.5cm) down from the top center of the slipper and make a mark. From that center mark, measure out 1½" (3.8cm) from each side of the slipper sole and mark. Create a half circle following the curve of the top of the slipper, connecting the two marks together. This half circle will follow the top half of the traced foot shape, but be slightly wider. Use this pattern for the slipper top.

3 Using the slipper templates (sole and slipper top), cut out the following pieces: 2 outer slipper tops from fabric, 2 lining

slipper tops from fabric, 2 slipper tops from cotton batting pieces, 2 soles from nonskid fabric, 2 soles from thick polyester batting, and 2 soles from lining fabric.

2 polyester batting pieces

2 outer slipper-top pieces

2 nonskid sole pieces

2 slipper cotton batting pieces

2 sole lining pieces

2 lining slipper-top pieces

4 Lay out both outer slipper-top and lining slipper-top fabric pieces and draw

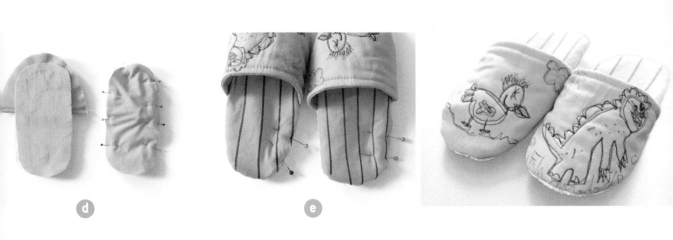

d

e

pictures on them. Create shapes, animals, lines—whatever you'd like! Allow the designs to dry completely and iron to heat-set them in place.

5 Layer the right sides of the slipper top and the lining top pieces together and then place the batting on top. Pin in place and sew along the straight edge. Fold the slipper top open and press the fold flat. Topstitch along the folded edge. Repeat for the second slipper top.

6 Free-motion quilt (page 24) or embroider parts of the drawn design to "quilt" the slipper top fabric and lining pieces together (b).

7 Layer the slipper sole pieces as follows: thick polyester batting; nonskid sole, right side up; quilted slipper top, right side down. Line up the edges, making sure they stay lined up around the curve of

the slipper top; it helps to pin the center together to keep the outer edges lined up (c). Then add the sole lining, wrong side up. Pin in place (d). Stitch around the entire slipper, leaving a small opening on the side for turning. Trim excess fabric ¼" (6mm) from the seam around the slipper and clip the curves. Turn right side out and press. Repeat for the other slipper.

8 Slip stitch the opening of the slipper closed (e).

read it together!

Shoes from Grandpa
by Mem Fox

Shoe-la-la!
by Karen Beaumont

The Foot Book
by Dr. Seuss

How Big Is a Foot?
by Rolf Myller

let's eat!

We love to eat. Who doesn't? But we particularly love to eat, cook, and garden together as a family. My husband is a nutritionist, so eating well is very important to our family. There aren't any foods that are necessarily off-limits, but we teach our kids moderation as they learn about better options. They're able to identify foods higher in nutrition versus those lower in nutrition, which they have abbreviated as "low-nu" and "high-nu."

Kids are never too young to spend time in the kitchen: give babies their own Tupperware drawer, teach younger children how to arrange placemats, and let older kids set the table. Cooking together and sitting together at the dinner table are great opportunities to give kids our attention. Frequent family meals are also associated with youngsters eating more fruits, vegetables, and fiber, as well as calcium- and vitamin-rich foods.

The projects in this chapter offer chances to bond over family mealtime. Softies make healthy eating and setting the table fun for younger children. Enjoy dinner over the placemats you made together, or go on a picnic with a special roll-up picnic blanket and admire the fabric combinations your child chose. I've also included a few easy kid-approved high-nu recipes in this chapter. When everyone's involved, meals are more memorable and vegetables more tasty (really!).

cheerful flip 'em placemats

These placemats not only protect the dinner table but will also make you smile when you see your child's artwork and your handiwork together. Mix or match fabric and embroidery on opposite sides so you can flip 'em over for a whole new look.

skill level

Sew Quick ☺

materials

Basic sewing supplies (page 12)

Eight 14" x 18" (35.5cm x 45.5cm) pieces of lightweight cotton fabrics for 4 placemats (use contrasting or coordinating fabrics for each side)

Four 14" x 18" (35.5cm x 45.5cm) pieces of cotton flannel fabrics (to give weight to the placemats)

Fabric markers

Embroidery hoop

Embroidery floss in colors to match fabric markers

seam allowance

½" (13mm)

finished measurements

13" x 17" (33cm x 43cm)

notes

• The placemats can be adjusted to fit your table. We have a vintage farm table, which is significantly smaller than regular dining tables, so these placemats are a wee bit smaller than the norm. A traditional placemat size is 13" x 19" (33cm x 48.5cm). If desired, adjust the size of the placemats to work best for your dining table, adding 1" (2.5cm) to the width and height for the seam allowance.

• To make coordinating cloth napkins, cut out large fabric squares, fold the edges under by ¼" (6mm) twice, and topstitch in place. You're all set for a lovely family dinner.

• Have each child design his or her own placemat for family meals—perhaps with a favorite fruit, favorite animal, or simply colorful shapes.

continues

1 With fabric markers, have your child draw a design on one corner of each placemat. (Leave the reversible side plain.) Be sure to let the design dry completely and iron to heat-set the designs in place.

2 Place the section of the placemat with the design in an embroidery hoop, and embroider (page 20) some parts of your child's design to give it more dimension.

3 Place the front and back fabrics together with right sides facing, place the cotton flannel on top, and sew around the perimeter of the placement, leaving a 3" (7.5cm) opening for turning. Clip the corners, turn inside out, and press. Repeat for each placemat.

4 Topstitch ¼" (6mm) from the edge around the entire placemat.

read it together!

Manners Can Be Fun
by Munro Leaf

Dinner with Olivia
by Emily Sollinger

Chato's Kitchen
by Gary Soto

prep & play place setting

Before you sit down to eat, make sure that you have everything set up for your guests. Children can learn how to set up a table properly with these softie versions of plates, forks, spoons, knives, and cups. When the meal is over, everything can be wrapped up neatly in the tablecloth bag.

skill level
Make in an Afternoon ⊙ ⊙

materials
Basic sewing supplies (page 12)

Prep & Play Place Setting template (page 169)

1⅜ yards (1.3m) total of various coordinating fabrics (makes 4 place settings)

1 yard (0.9m) of fabric for the tablecloth bag

1 yard (0.9m) of fabric for the bottom of the tablecloth bag

4" x 56" (10cm x 142cm) strip of fabric

1½ yards (1.4m) of cotton batting (1 yard [0.9m] is for the tablecloth bag and the remainder for the plates and cups)

Polyester fiberfill

String

Safety pin

seam allowance
½" (13mm)

finished measurement
Tablecloth bag is 30" (76cm) in diameter

note
For the play set pictured, there are 4 settings to allow for play with siblings and friends. To make more, just cut out all the necessary pieces first, then work through the process in an assembly line: cut, sew, stuff, and hand-sew them closed.

continues

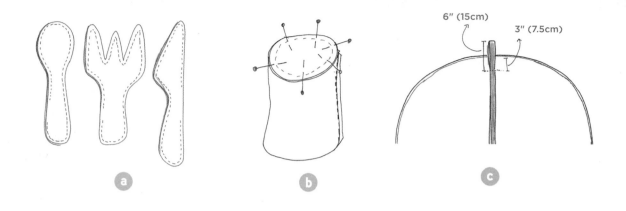

6" (15cm)   3" (7.5cm)

a   b   c

fork, spoon, and knife (make 4)

1 Using the template, cut out all pieces (front and back) for each utensil.

2 Place right sides together and stitch around the shapes, leaving a 1"–2" (2.5cm–5cm) opening as shown (a). Turn right side out. Stuff with polyester fiberfill, and slip stitch the opening closed. For the middle of the spoon, stitch an oval ¼" (6mm) from the top edge of the spoon.

cup (make 4)

1 Using the templates, cut out all pieces for the cup for a total of 6 pieces of fabric and batting: rectangular lining, rectangular exterior, rectangular batting, circular lining, circular exterior, circular batting. Cut out the 2 rectangular pieces on the bias.

2 Place the rectangular lining fabric right side down, and top with the rectangular batting. With right sides together, fold in half, lining up the short edges, and sew. This is the tube for the cup.

3 Place the lining circle right side down, and position the batting on top of the wrong side of the fabric, put right sides together (the circular piece and the sewn

teaching moments

On a piece of paper, draw out the proper position of the utensils in a place setting and have your child identify  each position. This paper guide helps to practice setting up the table, and can be used as a placemat for the Prep & Play Place Setting.

continues

tube), pin the circular piece and the tube together, and sew around the perimeter (b) of the circular piece. Clip around the curves to reduce bulk.

4 With the rectangular exterior fabric, place right sides together, lining up the short edges, and sew the short edges together.

5 With right sides together, pin the exterior circular fabric piece at the bottom of the tube created in step 4 and sew around the perimeter.

6 Place the outer fabric into the lining piece with their wrong sides together. Fold over ½" (13mm) and press. Fold over another ½" (13mm), pin, and sew ½" (13mm) from the edge. Turn inside out or leave as is. It's up to you which side you would like to use for the outer cup.

plate (make 4)

1 Using the template, cut out a total of 1 top fabric piece, 1 bottom fabric piece, and 2 batting pieces.

2 Lay out the plate fabrics. Layer them from bottom to top as follows: batting; top fabric, right side facing up; bottom fabric, right side facing down; batting. Sew around the perimeter, leaving 2" (5cm) open. Clip the curves. Turn, press, and slip stitch the opening closed. Topstitch the perimeter of the plate ½" (13mm) from the edge.

tablecloth bag

1 Cut out a 15" (38cm) length of string and tie it to a safety pin. Fold the fabric for the top of the tablecloth in half and attach the safety pin to the approximate center of the folded edge. Holding a fabric pencil at the end of the string, stretch the string and draw a half circle. Cut out and use this as a template to cut out the remaining piece of fabric for the bottom of the bag and the batting.

note
Use this moment to teach your child how to create a circle using a compass.

2 Place the right sides of the fabric together, with the layer of batting on top. Pin in place in various spots starting in the center to prevent any fabric movement and pulling. Sew a ½" (13mm) seam around and leave a 3" (7.5cm) opening. Clip the curves around the entire perimeter to reduce bulk, but be careful not to cut the stitching. Turn right side out, press, and slip stitch the opening closed. Edge stitch around the entire perimeter.

3 For the bag closure strap, fold the 4" x 56" (10cm x 142cm) strip of fabric in half lengthwise with the right sides together. Sew the entire length. Turn inside out, tuck in the open short edges ½" (13mm), and edge stitch the entire length of the strap on both long and short folded sides and press.

4 Fold the strap in half crosswise, measure 6" (15cm) down from the fold, and mark. Fold the tablecloth in half, mark 3" (7.5cm) down on the top center edge, and line up the mark on the strap with this mark on the tablecloth, and pin the strap in place. Open up the tablecloth and stitch the strap in place

(c). To close the bag, put all the utensils, cups, and plates in the center, gather the edges of the cloth together above them, and tie the strap around it in a bow. Use the loop as a bag handle for carrying when going from pretend picnic to pretend picnic.

---

feeding our children well

I'm thankful that my husband, Ben, was exposed early in our oldest daughter's life to what's known as the "division of responsibility in feeding" by Ellyn Satter, a trailblazing dietitian and social worker. Satter proposes a straightforward approach that we've adopted: when it comes to food and meals, parents and children have distinct roles:

The parent is responsible for *what*, *when*, and *where*.

The child is responsible for *how much* and *whether*.

In other words, parents need to provide our children with highly nutritious foods, but we must not force them to eat, as this can be counterproductive. Children are created with the ability to know how much to eat. Subduing the impulse to pressure our children into eating teaches them how to eat more intuitively. Easier said than done (as we well know), this approach takes courage. If your child says no, don't let that intimidate you, but be patient. Continue to provide them with healthful options. Be encouraged that, generally speaking, children may require five to twenty (or more) exposures to a food before they start to enjoy it. To learn more about how to provide a healthy environment for competent eaters, visit www.ellynsatterinstitute.org.

fill up with fruit & veggie softies

Now that we've set the table, let's fill up our plates with ripe fruits and veggies. One of the best things families can do together is to make—and enjoy—healthy food choices. Colorful play strawberries, pears, carrots, and tomatoes are not only good for you, but also easy to make. They can even be stitched by hand.

skill level
Sew Quick ⊚

materials
Basic sewing supplies (page 12)

Fill Up with Fruit & Veggie Softies template (page 169)

Various small scraps of fabric (¼ yard [23cm] makes at least 4 pieces of each fruit or veggie)

Scraps of green wool felt (¼ yard [23cm] of wool felt provides enough tops and leaves for 4 of each type of fruit and veggie)

Scrap of brown wool felt for the pear stems

Polyester fiberfill

Fabric glue

Embroidery floss (optional)

seam allowance
½" (13mm)

finished measurement
Pear is 7" (18cm) tall

notes
- Use patterned fabric for quirky softies: try a polka-dot tomato or a gingham strawberry.
- If you're in need of some "healthy"-size pillows to decorate a child's room, just enlarge the patterns even more to get gigantic fruit and vegetables.
- Stuffing the softies with polyester fiberfill is a good task for younger children.

continues

tomato

1 Using the template, cut 1 tomato top from wool felt. Cut out a circle of fabric 7½" (19cm) in diameter for the tomato body.

2 With the sewing machine set on the longest stitch (or with a running stitch by hand), stitch ¼" (6mm) from the edge around the entire perimeter of the circle. Backstitch at the very end.

3 Pull on the top thread to gather the fabric a bit (a).

4 Turn right side out and stuff with polyester fiberfill to desired firmness. Pull on the top thread again to gather the fabric tighter, make a couple stitches, and knot the thread to close the top of the tomato.

5 Add a bit of fabric glue to the wrong side of the tomato cap and attach it to the top of the tomato (b). The cap can also be hand-sewn on top and outlined with a running stitch around it.

note
You can use this pattern to make an apple as well. Instead of the tomato cap, cut leaves from the felt and make a stem with embroidery floss.

carrot

1 Using the template, cut out 2 pieces for the carrot body from fabric and 1 for the carrot top from wool felt.

2 With the right sides together, sew the length of both sides, and turn right side out.

3 With the sewing machine on the longest stitch (or with a running stitch by hand), stitch ¼" (6mm) from the edge around the top perimeter, and backstitch at the very end.

4 Pull on the top thread to gather up the fabric a bit. Stuff the carrot with polyester fiberfill to desired firmness.

5 Pull on the top thread again to gather the fabric tighter together, make a couple stitches, and knot the thread to close the top.

6 Wrap the leaves around the top of the carrot, adding fabric glue along the way to attach them.

teaching moments

• Create a rainbow using fruits and vegetables, and discuss what makes them so nutritious. Draw pictures of various fruits and vegetables that are represented by each color of the rainbow.

• Choose a new vegetable dish to try together. I've offered a few of our family's favorites (page 86).

strawberry

1 Using the template, cut out 1 strawberry body from fabric and 1 strawberry top from wool felt.

2 With the right sides together, fold the fabric in half so that the short raw edges are lined up with each other, and stitch along the entire short edge.

3 Set the sewing machine on the longest stitch (or with a running stitch by hand) and sew ¼" (6mm) from the edge along the curve. Backstitch at the very end.

4 Pull on the top thread to gather the fabric together, but leave a little opening.

5 Stuff the strawberry with polyester fiberfill. Pull on the thread to gather the fabric tighter, make a couple stitches, and knot the thread to close the top.

6 Add a bit of fabric glue to the wrong side of the strawberry cap and attach it to the top of the strawberry.

pear

1 Using the template, cut out 2 pear bodies from fabric and 1 pear leaf and 1 stem from wool felt.

2 Place the right sides of the pear together; insert the pear stem and leaf at the top center of one of the pear pieces, lining up the edge of both with the raw edge of the fabric (c). Sew around the perimeter of the pear, leaving a 2" (5cm) opening for turning. Clip all necessary curves.

3 Turn right side out and stuff with polyester fiberfill to desired firmness.

4 Slip stitch the opening to close.

tickled pink picnic blanket

When the kids are getting restless on a nice day, grab this rolled-up blanket and go on a picnic. Usually we're scrambling to find a blanket suitable for the adventure, but this designated one, with its little handle, makes it easy to pick up and go. No more last-minute hunting for a picnic blanket! We finally have the perfect one, and that tickles me pink.

skill level
Take Your Time ⊙ ⊙ ⊙

materials
Basic sewing supplies (page 12)

Twenty 15″ x 15″ (38cm x 38cm) squares of fabric

74″ x 60″ (188cm x 152.5cm) piece of fabric or twin-size bedsheet for backing

74″ x 60″ (188cm x 152.5cm) piece of thin cotton batting

1 yard (0.9m) of fabric for the bias tape binding

Bias tape maker (page 16)

11″ x 6″ (28cm x15cm) piece of fabric for the handle

40″ (101.5cm) piece of ½″- (13mm-) wide elastic

seam allowance
½″ (13mm)

finished measurements
57″ x 71″ (145cm x 180cm)

continues

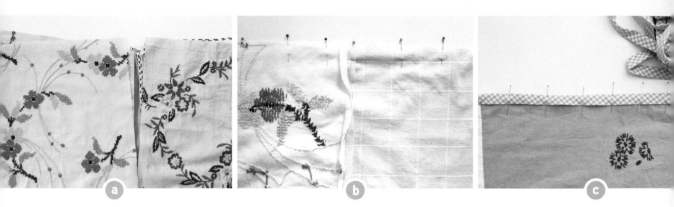

notes

- The key to simple quilt making is to use a lot of pins. Pinning is important to prevent movement and line up the squares as perfectly as possible.
- To make a waterproof picnic blanket, use a flannel fabric with a vinyl backing for the bottom, or replace the batting with a shower curtain and proceed to follow the project instructions.
- It is best to work on the quilt in a large open space with plenty of room to lay out all the pieces.

read it together!

The Bears' Picnic
by Stan and Jan Berenstain

One Hundred Hungry Ants
by Elinor J. Pinczes

A Picnic in October
by Eve Bunting

Mary Poppins in the Park
by P. L. Travers

1 Arrange the 15" x 15" (38cm x 38cm) fabric squares randomly or in an intentional pattern of 5 rows, with 4 squares in each row (a).

2 Gather the first row of 4 squares and place the first 2 squares with their right sides together, carefully lining up the edges perfectly. Pin in place and sew along one side to join. Continue to join the third square with the previous 2, then add the fourth square to the 3 sewn square patches. Press open all the seams and snip any excess thread. Repeat to make the remaining 4 rows.

3 Once all the squares are joined into rows, place the first 2 rows with their right sides together. Carefully line up the edges and pin them together (b).

note
Place a pin at the middle seam to help keep it aligned. Make sure the seams joining the

get out and go

Set aside some time to unplug from the TV or other digital distractions, and get outside. Go on a hike, plan a picnic, play at the beach, or simply take a walk around the neighborhood. Being outside and looking up reminds us how vast and wonderful our world is.

squares are matched up (or are really close; quirks are part of the beauty of a handmade quilt). Sew down the length of the entire long edge, snip any excess thread, and press the seams open. Continue to join the next rows (and press) until all 5 rows are sewn together.

4   Check the edges of the quilt and make sure that they are straight. (Again, some quirks are good in handmade things.) If there are any uneven edges, trim them slightly to make them straight.

5   Clear some space, then lay out the backing fabric with the wrong side up. Place the cotton batting on top, and center the front of the quilt, right side up, over the batting.

6   Leave 2" (5cm) of excess backing fabric and cotton batting on each side of the pieced quilt top and cut around it. Starting from the center and continually smoothing it along the way, pin all the quilt layers in place using a circular

pattern to prevent movement and slippage.

7   Sew all the layers together by stitching in the ditch (page 24) along all the seams of the quilt. Trim the excess batting and backing fabric so that the edges line up with the edges of the quilt top.

8   Make the bias tape binding (page 22). Pin the binding in place, and slip stitch the binding onto the quilt (c). The binding could also be machine-sewn on (which is faster), but I prefer the look of hand-sewn binding on a quilt. Press the entire quilt.

continues

9 To make the bag handle, fold the 11" x 6" (28cm x 15cm) piece of fabric in half with right sides together. Sew the entire length of the long edge, turn right side out, and press the seam open. Fold the short edges of the handle in ½" (13mm), press, and then edge stitch each long side of the handle.

10 Place the handle 5" (12.5cm) up from the bottom edge of the second square in the first row with the short end of the handle 3" (7.5cm) from each seam. Cut two lengths of elastic 20" (51cm) long. Fold the elastic in half, place the ends of each piece 1" (2.5cm) under the handle ½" (13mm) from the short edge, and pin in place (d). At the ends of the elastic loops, sew 1" (2.5cm) in and across to make a rectangle, then sew an X in the square, connecting each corner, to reinforce the handle.

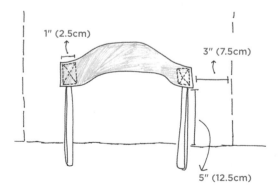

1" (2.5cm)

3" (7.5cm)

5" (12.5cm)

11 To roll up the picnic blanket, fold both long ends of the quilt top into the center. Fold again so that the quilt

is folded on top of the row with the handle. Roll from the opposite end up to the handle. Wrap the elastic loops around each side, grab it, and go!

---

book it

I highly recommend the book *The Family Dinner* by Laurie David (Grand Central, 2010). It's filled with lots of quick, basic recipes and loads of ideas to make your family dinners more intentional and memorable.

family time in the kitchen

Try a few of these ideas to help make cooking together special.

- Play some music. Set aside a few tunes as "dinnertime music" so that when you all hear it later, it will remind you of the time spent as a family in the kitchen.
- Have special aprons for your kitchen helpers.
- Talk about the food and which food groups they belong in. My husband is a dietitian, so there will always be a dialogue about food when he is in the kitchen cooking with the kids.
- Use this time to talk about his or her day. Tell your child your love story or your own childhood stories.
- Try new foods together. We talked about fennel and looked at pictures before actually purchasing some at a local farmer's market. The girls got excited immediately when they recognized it, and they loved it! I think part of the reason is the exposure they had to it prior to actually trying it.

recipes

best brussels sprouts ever SERVES 6

3 tablespoons extra-virgin olive oil

1½ pounds Brussels sprouts, ends trimmed, cut in half

⅔ cup vegetable stock

Zest from 1 lemon

1 tablespoon lemon juice

¼ teaspoon salt, or to taste

Pepper to taste

In a Dutch oven (or 8-quart stockpot), heat the olive oil over medium heat. Place the Brussels sprouts in a single layer, facedown, in contact with the heating surface, until they brown and caramelize nicely, around 4–5 minutes. Add vegetable stock and simmer for just another minute or so. Remove from the heat, mix in lemon zest, juice, and salt and pepper to taste. Serve immediately.

kale krispies SERVES 6

2 bunches curly kale (or dinosaur kale can be used as well)

Cooking spray

Salt to taste (or 1½ cups freshly grated Parmesan cheese)

Pepper to taste

Wash and dry the kale. Tear up the leaves into 2" (5cm) pieces. Lay them out, evenly spaced, on a baking sheet (lined with parchment paper if desired). Try not to overlap them or they will not cook evenly. Coat the kale with cooking spray. Sprinkle with salt and pepper (or cheese) to taste. Place in the oven at 275°F for about 18–20 minutes or until leaves are a deep green. The first time you try this recipe, monitor carefully in case they cook faster than you expect. The end result should be dry, crisp kale, without moist or pliable parts.

carrot fries SERVES 6

2 pounds large carrots (about 12), washed, peeled, and julienned into sticks about ¼" (6mm) thick x 4" (10cm) long

1 tablespoon extra-virgin olive oil

Salt and pepper to taste

Place the julienned carrots in a large bowl. Mix in the oil to coat. Sprinkle salt and pepper to taste. Lay them on a baking sheet close together, in a single layer so that they will bake evenly. (They may need to be divided into a few batches depending on the oven and size of the baking sheet.) Bake in the oven at 350°F for about 20 minutes.

our favorite picnic sandwich SERVES 6

Loaf of French bread

¼ cup soy mayonnaise

¼ cup honey Dijon mustard

4 ounces light Cheddar cheese

½ pound roast beef or other deli meat

4 cups spring greens

2 medium tomatoes, sliced

¼ onion, sliced

3 hard-boiled eggs, sliced

6 pickle slices

¼ tablespoon Italian dressing for drizzling

1 Cut the bread in half horizontally. Spread the mayo over the bottom half and the honey Dijon mustard on the top half.

2 Layer the cheese, roast beef (or other deli meat), spring greens, tomatoes, onions, eggs, and pickles on the bottom half of the bread.

3 Drizzle the top with the Italian dressing and place the remaining bread on top. Cut into 6 serving pieces and wrap each securely with parchment paper.

let's learn!

Children naturally know how to play hard, but teaching the "work hard" part takes a bit more practice and patience. Learning, working, and creating go hand in hand. Homeschooling allows me to integrate the skills I used when I was a teacher, and I love bringing lessons to life. After studying ancient Egypt, we created papier-mâché masks to mimic what King Tut's looked like. We learned about the sides of shapes, then read the book *The Greedy Triangle* as inspiration to create three-dimensional shapes with card stock. Making those connections took a history and math lesson one step further, and made for a memorable introduction to both topics.

The projects you'll find in this chapter seek ways to make learning more fun. Customize a lap pillow, zippered pencil case, or backpack to give your children a unique way to use and store school supplies. Turn a geography lesson into a keepsake world-map quilt made just for them, or use chore charts to hold them accountable and motivate them with a little incentive. Teaching kids isn't just the responsibility of their schools; parents can help reinforce lessons by doing things with them at home.

Our kids need to see us going about our daily work with joy, too. (If we're constantly complaining, our kids will pick up that attitude!) Show them how working hard and going the extra mile has many benefits.

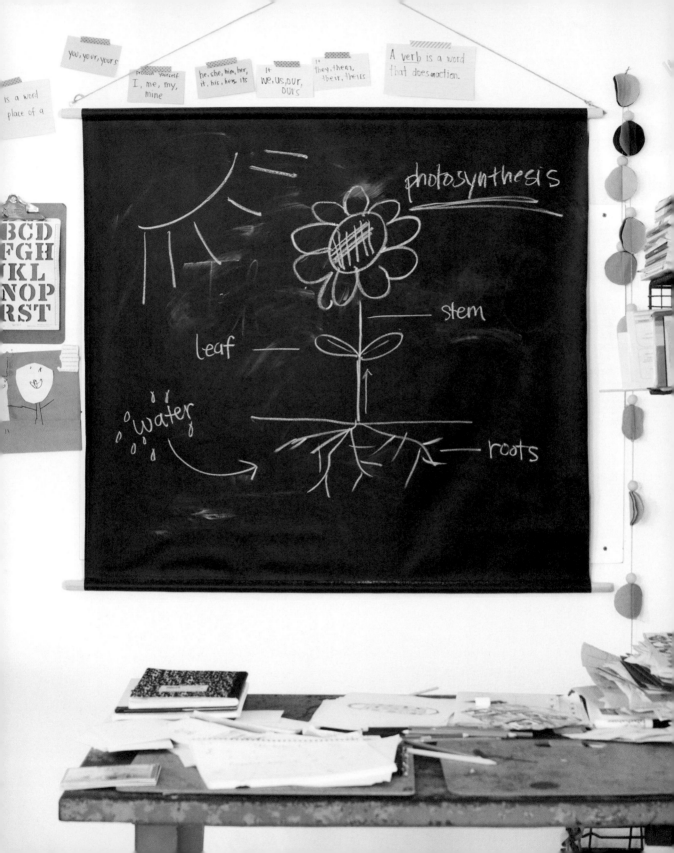

hanging chalkboard

Made with chalk cloth, this easy wall hanging can be a place to leave family messages, a center for learning, and a hub for creativity. We allow the kids to take turns drawing on our family chalkboard each month. Each child is always so proud when it's her work on display.

skill level
Sew Quick ⑪

materials
Basic sewing supplies (page 12)

47" x 45" (119.5cm x 114cm) piece of chalk cloth

Rolling sewing foot (for sewing on chalk cloth)

Two ¾" x 48" (2cm x 112cm) poplar dowels

Two 1⅛" (3cm) eye screws, ⅛" (3mm) in diameter

50" (127cm) length of twine or string

finished measurements
43" x 45" (110.5cm x 114cm)

1 Fold the top (shorter) edge of the chalk cloth under 2" (5cm), wrong sides together, and pin in place. Stitch 1½" (3.8cm) down from the folded edge to form the casing for the top dowel.

2 Fold the bottom edge of the chalk cloth (the opposite 45" [114cm] side) up 2" (5cm), wrong sides together, and pin in place. Stitch 1½" (3.8cm) from the folded edge to form the bottom casing.

3 Insert a dowel into each casing. On the top dowel, insert an eye screw 1" (2.5cm) from one end of the dowel. Repeat with the opposite end. Make sure the direction of the eye screws matches up symmetrically.

4 Tie the twine securely onto each of the eye screws, and hang your chalkboard.

comfy cozy lap pillow

It's cold out, and your kids want to stay warm in bed and doodle. A chalkboard inserted into the pocket creates a sturdy surface for reading, drawing, or journaling, which will be as comfortable as it is functional sitting on their laps. On a road trip, the chalkboard could be removed to create a travel pillow. The handles make it easy to grab and go.

skill level
Sew Quick ⊚

materials
Basic sewing supplies (page 12)

Two 4¼" x 10" (11cm x 25.5cm) pieces of fabric for the handle

Three 13" x 16" (33cm x 40.5cm) pieces of fabric for the pillow

Polyester fiberfill

9" x 12" (23cm x 30.5cm) chalkboard, whiteboard, or other hard surface

seam allowance
½" (13mm)

finished measurements
12" x 15" (30.5cm x 38cm), stuffed with polyester fiberfill

notes
• Change up the pillow by using 3 different fabrics, or simply keep them all the same. My daughter painted circles on one of the fabrics.

• It would be extra sweet if you embroidered the name of the pillow's owner in one corner.

continues

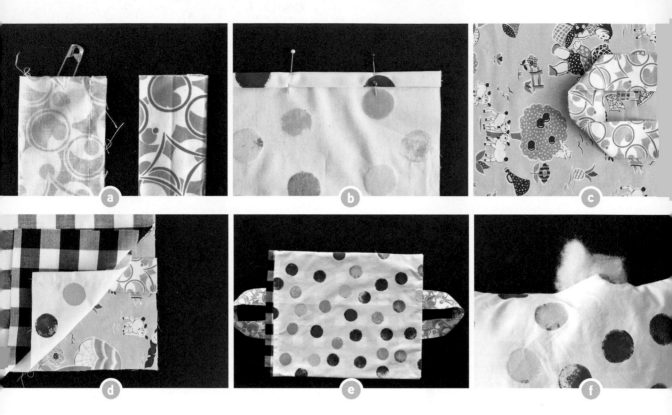

1 Make the handles by folding the 4¼" x 10" (11cm x 25.5cm) fabric pieces in half lengthwise with their right sides together. Sew the entire length along the raw edges. Turn inside out. Edge stitch both long sides of the strap (a).

2 Create the pocket for the insert with the top pillow fabric. Fold the top edge (one shorter side) down ½" (13mm) and press. Fold down again ½" (13mm) and press. Pin in place, then topstitch ½" (13mm) from the edge (b).

3 Lay the bottom pillow fabric right side up, center the straps on the shorter side 3½" (9cm) in from each side; repeat for the opposite end (c). Place the pocket fabric right side down on top of the straps, then place the bottom fabric right side down. Pin in place (d). Stitch around, leaving a 3" (7.5cm) opening. Clip the corners, turn, and press (e).

4 Fill the pillow with fiberfill, and slip stitch the opening closed (f). Insert a chalkboard, whiteboard, or large book into the pocket to provide a sturdy surface for reading, writing, or drawing.

get-it-done chore chart

Use this chart to help your children keep track of their responsibilities and see their accomplishments. Kids need to be given chances to display responsibility so they can learn how to actively contribute to the ebb and flow of the family. And everyone wants to earn a gold star!

skill level
Make in an Afternoon ⊚ ⊚

materials
Basic sewing supplies (page 12)

23" x 37" (58.5cm x 94cm) piece of utility fabric or heavy interfacing

Two 23" x 37" (58.5cm x 94cm) pieces of fabric for the back and front of the pocket chart

Eight 2" x 22" (5cm x 56cm) pieces of clear vinyl

One $5/16$" x 24" (8mm x 61cm) dowel

32" (81cm) length of twine or string

seam allowance
½" (13mm)

finished measurements
21½" x 35" (54.5cm x 89cm)

note
I used utility fabric between the fabrics to give the chart weight, but fusible interfacing will give it that same structure.

continues

1 Layer fabric as follows: utility fabric; back fabric, right side up; top fabric (front of chart), right side down. Pin the layers together and sew 3 sides of the rectangle, but leave the bottom edge open. Clip the corners at an angle to reduce bulk. Turn inside out and press if needed.

read it together!

The Berenstain Bears and the Trouble with Chores
by Stan and Jan Berenstain

How Do Dinosaurs Clean Their Rooms?
by Jane Yolen and Mark Teague

Clifford's Spring Clean-Up
by Norman Bridwell

A Day's Work
by Eve Bunting

2 Fold the bottom in 1" (2.5cm) and sew ½" (13mm) from the edge.

3 Place the first strip of vinyl 3" (7.5cm) from the top and pin in place. Place the remaining strips 2" (5cm) apart and pin in place.

4 Topstitch the entire length of the chart ½" (13mm) from the edge, sewing down the vinyl strips on the side. Repeat with the opposite side.

5 Sew across the bottom of each row of vinyl.

6 Fold the top 1" (2.5cm) down to the back and edge stitch at the bottom (a).

7 Feed the dowel through the casing at the top, and tie the twine or string to each end.

travel the world quilt

Take your children on a trip around the world while they snuggle under this playful quilt to read books about different countries and cultures. This appliquéd quilt is easier to make than it might look at first glance, thanks to the magic of fusible web that helps stabilize each shape as you stitch.

skill level

Take Your Time ⊕ ⊕ ⊕

materials

Basic sewing supplies (page 12)

Travel the World Quilt template (page 170)

Pencil

1¼ yard (1.1m) of lightweight fusible web

Various fabric scraps for the appliqués (my quilt used 8 different patterned fabrics, for a total of 1¼ yards [1.1m] of fabric; the largest piece is approximately 17" x 21" [43cm x 53.5cm])

40" x 53" (101.5cm x 134.5cm) piece of fabric for the front background

1½ yards (1.4m) of fabric for the backing

1½ yards (1.4m) of cotton batting

Free-motion quilting foot (optional)

Yardstick or ruler and straightedge

1 yard (0.9m) of fabric for bias tape binding

Bias tape maker (page 16)

seam allowance

½" (13mm)

finished measurements

40" x 52½" (101.5cm x 133cm)

notes

- The size of the actual quilt is slightly larger than the template, so spread out the countries using a real map as reference to fill the space.
- The countries can be appliquéd (page 22) or attached with free-motion quilting (page 24).

continues

1 Enlarge the template and trace each piece with a pencil onto the paper backing of the fusible web.

2 Cut out each shape with a ¼" (6mm) allowance around the edges.

3 Place the fusible web, with the fusible web side down, onto the wrong side of the appliqué fabric and fuse the web to the fabric following the manufacturer's instructions.

teaching moments

- Make flags for the various countries on the quilt and pin them in place.
- Make special markers for places you have visited as a family.
- Identify all the continents. How many countries can you name?

4 Cut along the pencil markings on the paper backing, and remove the paper backing.

5 Place each appliqué piece in its correct spot on the front background fabric. Pin the appliqué securely to prevent any further movement (a). Zigzag-stitch each piece in place by sewing around its entire perimeter. For shorter pieces, use a shorter stitch length, and use a longer stitch for the larger pieces. For the tiny islands (b), free-motion quilt (page 24) each piece or sew it on by hand using a running stitch.

6 With an air-fading marker and starting from the top left corner of the quilt, make marks every 4" (10cm) all the way to the bottom. Using the marks as a guide and a long straightedge, draw a straight line that goes horizontally across the quilt from the left- to the right-hand side. Repeat this every 4" (10cm), creating horizontal lines from the top to the bottom of the quilt.

7 Mark the center top of the quilt with the air-fading marker and draw a straight line vertically down the middle of the quilt. Proceed to mark two dots 3" (7.5cm) away from the center line on both sides, then two lines 7" (18cm), 11" (28cm), 16" (40.5cm), and 22" (56cm) from the center line. Repeat these markings for the bottom of the quilt.

8 Draw slightly curved lines, connecting the top mark to its corresponding bottom mark. These curved lines give the appearance of longitude lines as represented on some world maps.

9 Place the backing fabric wrong side up, place the cotton batting on top, and center the front background fabric on top, with its right side facing up.

10 Leaving an excess of 2" (5cm) of backing fabric and cotton batting around the entire quilt, cut off the remaining edges.

11 Starting at the center of the quilt, pin all the layers together, moving in a circular motion outward and smoothing the quilt as you go, to prevent movement and slippage.

12 Starting at the center top line, straight-stitch down the quilt through all the layers. Working from the center out, continue to straight-stitch through each drawn line to join all the pieces until all the drawn lines have been stitched. Cut any excess threads.

13 Make 1" (2.5cm) bias tape binding (page 22) and hand-sew it onto the entire perimeter of the quilt (c). The binding can also be machine-sewn, but I find that hand-sewing always yields the best result.

read it together!

Oh, the Places You'll Go!
by Dr. Seuss

Around the World with Mouk
by Marc Boutavant

Around the World in Eighty Days
by Jules Verne

Gulliver's Travels
by Jonathan Swift

The Travels of Babar
by Jean de Brunhoff

Babar Comes to America
by Laurent de Brunhoff

Madeline
by Ludwig Bemelmans

This Is London
by Miroslav Sasek

This Is Rome
by Miroslav Sasek

storytelling box

I remember coming up with this idea when I was a kid, dreaming of becoming an animator. Kids can create their own "cartoon" with a few inexpensive materials on a rainy afternoon.

materials

Shoe box and lid

Ruler

Scissors

60" (152.5cm) strip of paper with a height that fits in your shoe box (you may need to tape multiple pieces of paper together)

Markers or colored pencils

Two $^{3}\!/_{16}$" x 12" (5mm x 30.5cm) wooden dowels

Masking tape

1 Use a ruler to help you mark and cut out a rectangle from the shoe box lid. Leave at least a 1" (2.5cm) frame around, which acts as a window around the cartoon.

2 Measure the height of the shoe box lid and subtract 1" (2.5cm). Cut the 60"- (152.5cm-) long strip of paper to this height.

3 Measure the width of the window on the shoe box lid, and use that measurement to lightly mark the paper strip with each separate frame that will be shown in the window.

4 Allow your child to create a story with markers or colored pencils. Teach him or her that the story will progress from left to right and each frame should have a different part of the story.

5 With scissors, poke a hole ½" (13mm) in from the short edge and centered on the top of the box.

Repeat for the other side. Proceed to poke holes at the bottom directly underneath the top 2 holes.

6 Once each frame has been completed, insert the dowels through the holes and make sure they are even and parallel with each other. Tape the short edge of the right side of the strip to the right dowel and roll the strip onto the right dowel until there is one story frame left in the window. Then proceed to tape the remaining side onto the second dowel. The story will be shared as the storyteller rolls the dowels. Place the shoe box lid on the box.

silly, silly cuckoo clock

What time is it? It's time to make this kid-friendly clock—which really works! When they finally learn how to tell time, your children will look up at this clock hanging on the wall and smile. It's playful and different from any clock out there, perfect in a child's room or as a gift for a baby nursery.

skill level
Make in an Afternoon ⊞ ⊞

materials
Basic sewing supplies (page 12)

Silly, Silly Cuckoo Clock template (page 171)

¼ yard (23cm) of patterned fabric for the front and back of the house

Two 3½" x 6" (9cm x 15cm) pieces of fabric for the clock sides

Two 3½" x 9" (9cm x 23cm) pieces of fabric for the clock roof

10" (25.5cm) square of solid-colored fabric for the clock face

½ yard (45.5cm) of heavy interfacing

5" (12.5cm) piece of felt fabric for the bird

5" (12.5cm) piece of fabric (or felt fabric) for the twig

Embroidery hoop

Embroidery floss

Buttonhole foot

Battery-operated clock parts

2 pom-poms (page 33)

28" (71cm) length of yarn to match the pom-poms

Safety pin (optional)

seam allowance
½" (13mm)

finished measurements
9" x 10½" x 2½" (23cm x 26.5cm x 6.5cm)

continues

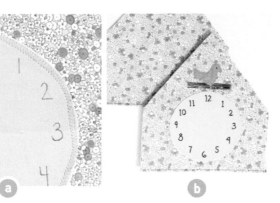

notes

- Make the clock colorful by using different patterned fabrics for the different parts of the house.
- To make a nonworking clock for learning and playtime, create clock arms using wool felt and use a brad to allow arm movement.

1 Using the template, cut out 2 house shapes from fabric and 2 house shapes from interfacing. Continue to cut out all the remaining pieces for the cuckoo clock, except the clock face.

note

Each fabric piece, except the clock face, goes with a corresponding piece of interfacing.

2 With an air-fading maker, draw a 6"- (15cm-) diameter circle on the clock-face fabric and write the numbers (a).

3 Place the portion of the clock face in an embroidery hoop and use a backstitch (page 20) to embroider the numbers on the clock face. Cut out the clock face.

4 Place the clock face right side up on the right side of the front fabric and appliqué to the front using a zigzag stitch.

5 Appliqué the bird and twig above the clock face either by hand or with a zigzag stitch (b).

6 Fuse the interfacing to the wrong side of all the fabric pieces.

7 Fold under the bottom of the front, back, and side fabrics by ½" (13mm), pin, and topstitch the entire length of each piece ¼" (6mm) from the edge.

8 Using the button-hole foot, make a buttonhole centered on the back fabric 3½" (9cm) down from the top.

3½" (9cm)

9 With their right sides together, sew the short side of the left side fabric to the short side of the left roof fabric. Repeat for the right side. Press the seams open.

10 Place the left side piece and front fabric with their right sides together. Align the edges to the front fabric, making sure to line up the topstitched bottoms. Pin in place and sew the entire length. Repeat this step again for the right side and front fabric pieces.

11 Attach the back fabric to the left side piece with their right sides together, line up the raw edges of the long side to the house fabric, making sure to line up the topstitched bottoms, pin in place, and sew the entire length. Repeat this step again for the right side and back fabric pieces (c).

12 With the cuckoo clock still wrong side out and right sides together, sew the top roof pieces together from the front tip of the cuckoo clock to the back tip of the cuckoo clock 1" (2.5cm) down from the top raw edge (d). Clip all corners and turn the cuckoo clock right side out.

13 Cut a small hole in the center of the clock face and attach the clock parts following the package instructions.

14 Attach 2 pom-poms to each end of a 28" (71cm) piece of yarn, and attach the center of the yarn to the seam allowance inside the cuckoo clock by hand-sewing or simply using a safety pin to secure it to the top center seam.

read it together!

Telling Time with Big Mama Cat
by Dan Harper

The Clock Struck One
by Trudy Harris

Clocks and More Clocks
by Pat Hutchins

Thirteen O'Clock
by James Stimson

When It's Six O'Clock in San Francisco
by Cynthia Jaynes Omololu

Time Zones
by David A. Adler

their artwork zippered pouch

As a kid, I was a pencil fanatic, collecting every color, and my kids are the same way. This zippered clutch featuring their own personal artwork will no doubt be a treasured spot for their pencil collections. It's also a great introduction to sewing zippers; once you've mastered the technique, you'll find all kinds of uses for them.

skill level
Make in an Afternoon ☺ ☺

materials
Basic sewing supplies (page 12)

Two 4½" x 10" (11.5cm x 25.5cm) pieces of light-colored fabric for the top exterior

Two 3½" x 10" (9cm x 25.5cm) pieces of fabric for the bottom exterior

Two 7" x 10" (18cm x 25.5cm) pieces of lining fabric

Fabric markers or fabric paint and paintbrushes

10" (25.5cm) zipper

seam allowance
½" (13mm)

finished measurements
Approximately 6½" x 9" (16.5cm x 23cm)

notes
- This pouch can be made in any size; make it small to be a wallet or large enough to hold an iPad.
- Add fringe or a pom-pom (page 33) to the end of the zipper pull for extra embellishment.
- To use your child's existing artwork, print it onto an iron-on transfer (page 15), then iron the transfer onto a piece of fabric. Keep in mind that the image will be mirrored.

continues

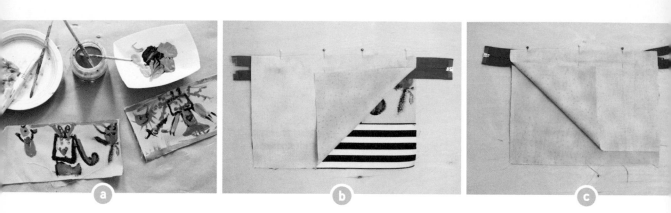

1 Using fabric markers or fabric paint, let your child create a piece of art on both exterior fabric pieces. Allow the artwork to completely dry and heat-set it (a).

2 Place the bottom exterior fabric and the top exterior fabric together with their right sides together, lining up the edges of the 10" (25.5cm) side. Pin and edge stitch in place. Repeat with the remaining top and bottom exterior fabric. Once the bottom of the exterior fabric and the top exterior fabric are sewn together, the dimensions of the exterior fabric should be 7" x 10" (18cm x 25.5cm), which is the same as the lining fabric. Press the seams open.

3 Place the entire exterior piece right side up, lay the zipper on the 10" (25.5cm) side edge with the teeth side down on top (make sure the zipper pull is on the left), and place the lining fabric right side down on top of the zipper. Making sure that the fabric and zipper edges are lined up, pin in place (b). Start 1" (2.5cm) away from the zipper pull and sew ¼" (6mm) from the edge of the fabric. Pull the zipper pull down to avoid it getting caught and sew the remaining 1" (2.5cm) edge. Flip the fabrics so that the wrong sides are facing, and press.

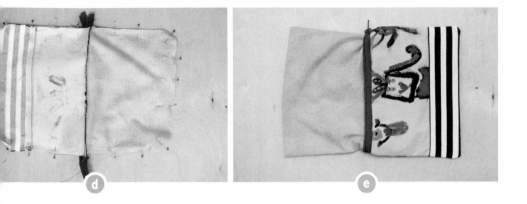

4 Place the remaining exterior fabric right side up; lay the zipper (with the fabrics attached) on top, with the teeth side facing down and the zipper pull on the right. Place the lining fabric on top with the right side facing down. Pin in place (c). Sew ¼" (6mm) from the edge of the fabric, stopping short 1" (2.5cm) from the zipper pull. Pull the zipper away from the edge to prevent it from getting caught and continue to stitch along the remaining edge. Place the wrong sides together and press.

5 Open up the fabrics so that the exterior pieces are right sides together and the lining pieces are right sides together. Pin in place. The zipper will be in the middle (d).

6 Sew around all the edges using a ½" (13mm) seam allowance, but leave a 3"

(7.5cm) opening at the bottom of the lining fabric. Clip the corners to reduce bulk, being careful not to cut the seam.

7 Unzip the zipper and push the fabrics through the 3" (7.5cm) opening so that the right sides are out. Sew the opening in the lining fabric closed using either a slip stitch or edge stitch as close to the edge as possible. Press the lining fabric and push it into the clutch (e).

family sketchbooks

We have a big sketchbook on our coffee table next to a container of colored pencils. Our kids will draw in it, we'll draw together as a family, and so will visitors to the house. At the beginning of the year, we replace the old one with a new one and date it. They are fun to look back at to see how our children's drawings have changed and what we've done together.

clever appliqué backpacks

Send them on their merry way wearing a personalized backpack. Stuff it with school or sports practice items. Either way, this bag is perfect for toting around the little ones' little things and can be decked out with any simple appliqué motif they can dream up. I would wear the *lucha libre* one myself!

skill level

Take Your Time ⊕ ⊕ ⊕

materials

Basic sewing supplies (page 12)

Clever Appliqué Backpack template (page 171)

8" x 10" (20.5cm x 25.5cm) piece of double-faced fusible interfacing

8" x 10" (20.5cm x 25.5cm) piece of fabric for apple or mask appliqué

Two 13" x 15" (33cm x 38cm) pieces of heavyweight fabric for the front and back

Two 5" x 12" (12.5cm x 30.5cm) pieces of fabric for the flap

Four 4" x 15½" (10cm x 39.5cm) pieces of fabric for the straps (to match the appliqué)

Two 13" x 15" (33cm x 38cm) pieces of fabric for the lining

Fabric paint and paintbrushes (for the mask only)

Buttonhole foot

Two 1" (2.5cm) buttons

seam allowance

½" (13mm)

finished measurements

12" x 14½" (30.5cm x 37cm)

notes

• Try drawing your own motif.

• Omit the bottom straps to make a tote instead of a backpack.

continues

1 Fuse the lightweight interfacing onto the fabric that will be used for the apple or mask. Using the template, cut out an apple and leaf (or mask). Use a different fabric for the leaf or layer a different fabric underneath the mask, if you want some variety. Center the apple/mask with its right side facing up on the right side of the front fabric and pin in place. Appliqué the apple/mask onto the fabric by fusing the motif onto the fabric (page 22), then secure around the edges with a zigzag stitch (a). The mask will also require the inside of the eye, nose, and mouth holes to be zigzag-stitched, ensuring that the mask is securely attached to the background.

for the mask only
With some fabric paint and a paintbrush, outline the face mask to define it further. Allow your child to paint on any extra designs if desired. Make sure the paint dries completely and press to heat-set it (b).

2 Fold the straps in half lengthwise with right sides together and sew around the perimeter of the strap, leaving one short end open. Repeat with the remaining 3 strap pieces. Turn inside out and press. Edge stitch all strap pieces (c).

3 Place the right sides of the flap fabric together, and stitch around 3 sides, leaving one long side open. Turn and press. Edge stitch around the 3 sewn sides. Using a buttonhole foot, make a buttonhole ½" (13mm) up from the sewn edge of the flap and 1" (2.5cm) in from the side. Repeat with the opposite side (d).

4 Place the exterior fabric (with motif) right side up, and next place the 2 straps on the bottom of the fabric 2" (5cm) in from the side edge. With the fabric edges lined up on the bottom, place the remaining exterior fabric on top with the right side down. Pin in place and sew around 3 sides of the bag, leaving the top open (e). Clip corners.

5 Place the lining fabric right sides together, pin in place, and sew around the 3 sides, leaving the top open. Clip corners to reduce bulk.

6 With the right sides together, place the exterior bag into the lining bag. Place the 2 top straps between the exterior fabric and lining 2" (5cm) in from each side with the fabric edges lined up. Place the bag flap on top of the straps, lining up the raw edges of the flap, the straps, and exterior fabric, with right sides together. The top straps and bag flap are sandwiched between the exterior bag fabric and the lining bag fabric. Pin in place and sew around, leaving a 3" (7.5cm) opening for turning. Turn inside out and press. Fold in the remaining opening, press, and edge stitch around the entire perimeter of the top.

7 Line the buttons up with the buttonholes on the front exterior fabric and hand-sew them in place (f). Tie the straps together at a length that's comfortable for your child to wear.

let's play!

Children are filled with boundless energy and imagination. They can turn a roll of wrapping paper into a wand, a bathmat into a flying carpet, and a dining table into a fairy-tale castle. Sometimes they will play with a plain box longer than the toys already sitting in their room! Kids don't need the bells and whistles of electronic toys to have fun. Often times, my girls will come up to me with a gazillion ideas for things to make from simple items lying around the house. It's so fun to watch them be little inventors.

In their minds, puppets can be used to tell a story, pillows can be dollhouses, and robots can fly. This chapter is filled with simple toys that show kids the endless possibilities they can create with their imaginations and a few simple supplies. You'll also find ideas for theatrical perform-ances, writing prompts, and other activities inspired by the projects.

Hands-on playtime activities are essential to childhood. I vividly remember how I just loved the feeling of working on a project and being able to enjoy the finished product. (I'm also thankful that my parents let me turn the house upside down with my creative projects.) I now have the privilege of sharing that sense of accomplishment through sewing and drawing inspiration from my daughters' wild imaginations!

★ The BOX Puppet ★ *Theater*

big box theater troupe

Ladies and gentlemen, we now present . . . the first of many fabulous puppet performances! This reversible two-characters-in-one puppet will take center stage, and the theater's working curtains (customizable for any size stage) will unveil a full afternoon of family matinees.

skill level
Make in an Afternoon ☺ ☺

materials
Basic sewing supplies (page 12)

Whimsical Topsy-Turvy Puppet template (page 171)

Four 14" x 10" (35.5cm x 25.5cm) pieces of coordinating fabrics for the puppet body (2 for each puppet)

Four 6" x 6" (15cm x 15cm) squares of light-colored solid fabrics for the puppet heads and bodies (use a different shade for each character if desired, 2 of each color)

Two 6" x 6" (15cm x 15cm) squares of wool felt for the puppet hair (use a different color for each character)

Fabric paint and paintbrushes

Polyester fiberfill

Large box with 4 intact flaps

Cellophane or duct tape

Ruler

Scissors

½ yard (45.5cm) of fabric for an 18" (45.5cm) square box

Wooden dowel, 2" (5cm) longer than the width of the box

seam allowance
½" (13mm)

finished measurements
Puppet is 9" x 12" (23cm x 30.5cm)

notes
- Kids can create more characters by painting or drawing other faces. Use the head shape as the base, and feel free to add your own type of hair and ears, too.
- Decorate the outside of the box with stripes or polka dots! Use the space on the box flap to create a title for your personal theater.
- You can make the curtains longer if you want them to reach the bottom of the box.

continues

1 Using the template, cut out all the necessary pieces: 2 Strong Man body pieces, 2 Strong Man head (and coordinating hair) pieces, 2 Clumsy Clown body pieces, and 2 Clumsy Clown head (and coordinating hair) pieces.

for the Strong Man
Edge stitch the wool-felt hair onto both the front and back head fabric.

2 Paint the faces on both the front head pieces for the Strong Man and Clumsy Clown (a). Allow the faces to dry completely, and press to heat-set them. Also paint the striped design on the

Strong Man's body piece, allow it to dry completely, and heat-set (b).

3 Place the Strong Man body pieces with their right sides together, and stitch around the perimeter, leaving the bottom and top completely open.

4 Place the Clumsy Clown fabric interior body pieces with their right sides together, and stitch around the perimeter, leaving the bottom and top completely open.

5 Place the Clumsy Clown body and the Strong Man body pieces with their wrong sides together. Fold the bottom of each puppet body under ½" (13mm), press, and pin. Edge stitch around the entire bottom perimeter (c).

6 To assemble the heads, place both front face pieces of the Strong Man and

read it together!

If I Ran the Circus
by Dr. Seuss

Olivia Saves the Circus
by Ian Falconer

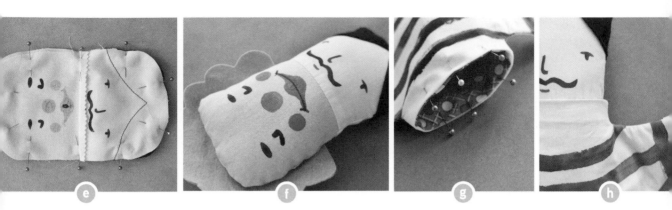

Clumsy Clown with their right sides together and pin in place. Stitch the base of the heads together. Press the seam open.

7 Place the backing head pieces of the Strong Man and Clumsy Clown with their right sides together, pin in place, and stitch the base of the heads together. Press the seam open (d).

8 Place the front and back heads with their right sides together. Make sure the Strong Man face is facing its corresponding back of the head, and the same with the Clumsy Clown. Pin in place, stitch around, and leave a 2" (5cm) opening for turning (e). Clip curves and corners. Turn right side out and press.

9 Lightly stuff the puppet head with polyester fiberfill. Don't overstuff it

because you want to make sure there will be room in the puppet body for your child to insert his or her hand.

10 Hand-stitch the Clumsy Clown wool-felt hair piece onto the back of the Clumsy Clown head (f).

11 Fold the entire neckline of the puppet body in ½" (13mm) and press (g).

12 Insert the puppet head into the puppet body, aligning it at the neckline and making sure to correspond the correct body to the correct head. By hand, slip stitch the neckline onto the puppet head (h).

13 Fold all but one of the box flaps in. Tape the two sides of the remaining flap to the box to keep the flap upright; this will be the bottom of the theater.

continues

14 On the sides of the box, measure 1" (2.5cm) down from the top and 1" (2.5cm) in from the edge and mark with an X. Repeat on the opposite side.

15 With scissors, cut a slit on each line of the marked X, and be sure to cut through all layers. This is where the dowel will be inserted for the curtain.

16 Measure the width and height of the box's window opening. Divide the width measurement in half and add an extra 5" (12.5cm). Add 5" (12.5cm) to the existing length of the opening for the curtain length. Write these measurements down, and then cut out 2 curtain panels using these measurements.

17 Turn in both side edges of one curtain ¼" (6mm), press; fold over another ¼" (6mm), press again, and pin in place. Edge stitch the entire length of the sides. Repeat for the second curtain panel.

18 Hem both curtain pieces by folding the bottom up ¼" (6mm), press; fold up ¼" (6mm) again, press, and pin in place. Stitch the hem in place.

19 At the top edge of each curtain, fold down ½" (13mm), press; fold down 1½" (3.8cm), press, and pin in place. Edge stitch the top panel of the curtain.

20 Insert the dowel through one end of the box, slip both curtain panels on, and continue feeding the dowel through the remaining hole on the opposite side.

read it together!

Not a Box
by Antoinette Portis

A Box Story
by Kenneth Kit Lamug

The True Story of the Three Little Pigs
by Jon Scieszka

funny family glove puppets

When winter comes, stock up on knit gloves. These can easily be turned into a family of no-sew glove puppets.

materials
Knit gloves
Craft glue
Ten 5mm wiggle eyes
Scissors
Various scraps of wool felt

Glue a pair of wiggle eyes on each glove finger. Cut out different hats, hairstyles, or other face details from wool felt and glue them onto each glove finger. Make the family funny or colorful, or make them all animals. Once each glove finger is completed and the glue has dried, have your child tell you a story using his or her new characters.

quirky rag doll

A child can never have too many dolls, and I think this special one is begging to be added to the collection. With her sweet yarn hair, this little gal has a lot of steps; but it's worth the extra time to master the basics of doll making. Try using an unexpected color combination for the doll body and dress to add extra personality to your special rag doll.

skill level
Take Your Time ◉ ◉ ◉

materials
Basic sewing supplies (page 12)

Quirky Rag Doll template (page 172)

¼ yard (23cm) of patterned fabric for the doll's body

¼ yard (23cm) of contrasting patterned fabric for the doll's dress

Polyester fiberfill

Yarn for the hair

12" (30.5cm) piece of cardboard or book

Tape

Tissue paper

Embroidery floss for the eyes

Scrap of pink wool felt for the mouth

Pink fabric paint and paintbrush for the cheeks

Two 6" (15cm) pieces of fabric or ribbon for tying pigtails

seam allowance
½" (13mm)

finished measurement
22" (56cm) tall

note
The doll's face is made with a bit of wool felt, embroidery floss, and hand painting, but it can also be entirely hand-painted or hand-sewn. The little details you add to personalize the doll will make her even more special.

continues

doll

1 Using the template, cut out all the pattern pieces for the rag doll's body from the patterned fabric: 4 arm pieces, 4 leg pieces, and 2 body pieces.

2 Pin 2 arm pieces together with their right sides facing and sew around the perimeter, but make sure to leave the base open. Turn and press. Repeat for the second pair of arm pieces.

3 Pin 2 leg pieces together with their right sides facing and sew around the perimeter, making sure to leave the base open. Turn and press. Repeat for the second pair of leg pieces.

4 Pin the 2 body pieces together with their right sides facing, sew around the perimeter, but make sure to leave the base open. Clip the curves, then turn and press (a).

5 Stuff the arm, leg, and body pieces with polyester fiberfill to the desired thickness (b).

6 Fold the base of the body in ½" (13mm) and press. Insert the legs ½" (13mm) into the base of the body, with each leg ½" (13mm) from the corner of the body. Pin in place and edge stitch the opening closed (c).

7 Fold the opening of the arms ½" (13mm) and hand-sew onto the body

read it together!

Babushka's Doll
by Patricia Polacco

The Best-Loved Doll
by Rebecca Caudill

using a whip stitch. Repeat with the remaining arm (d).

rag-doll yarn hair

1 Wind the yarn around a piece of cardboard or book about 12" (30.5cm) wide approximately 70 times (e).

2 Cut a piece of tape the entire width of the yarn and add 2" (5cm). Press the tape onto the side of the yarn (f). Repeat with the other side of the yarn. Cut the yarn at the bottom and top of the cardboard to release the yarn.

3 Using a piece of tissue paper the same length as the tape, place the yarn on top of the tissue paper and evenly spread out the yarn, leaving no gaps between each strand of yarn. Use the tape to secure the yarn down onto the tissue paper (g).

4 Using thread the same color as the hair, zigzag-stitch down the center of the hair (h). Remove the tape and tissue paper, and you've just made rag-doll hair!

face and hair

1 Mark the placement of the eyes and rosy cheeks with an air-fading marker. Create the eyes with embroidery floss and a single running stitch.

2 Cut out a tiny heart from pink wool felt or fabric and hand-sew it onto the face for the lips.

3 Create the rosy cheeks by painting two circles with fabric paint. Allow the paint to dry completely, and heat-set it (i).

4 Place the hair on the head, pin in place, and hand-sew it onto the head all

continues

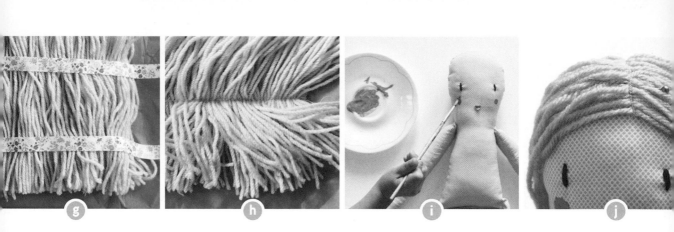

the way down to where the doll's ears would be (j).

note
Hold down all the hair as you stitch it onto the head to prevent hair strands from getting caught in the stitching.

5 Gather the hair into two low pigtails and use a 6" (15cm) piece of fabric or ribbon to tie each pigtail. Trim the yarn strands to make sure the hair is even (k).

dress

1 Using the template, cut out all the dress pattern pieces from the contrasting patterned fabric: 2 panel pieces and a strip of fabric 1½" x 24" (3.8cm x 61cm) (l).

2 Fold one arm opening under ¼" (6mm), press; fold under another ¼" (6mm), press, and pin in place. Topstitch

the entire length of the seam. Repeat for the arm opening of the second dress panel (m).

3 With right sides together, pin the sides of the panels, making sure the armholes are lined up. Starting at the top, stitch the panels together. Repeat for the other side of the dress. Turn the dress right side out and press.

4 Take the long fabric strip, fold each long side under ¼" (6mm), press; fold ¼" (6mm) under on each side again toward the center and press.

5 Now fold the fabric strip in half crosswise, and ½" (13mm) from the folded edge, sandwich the front and

back neckline between the folded edges of the fabric strip. Pin in place.

6 Fold in both ends of the strip ¼" (6mm) and pin. Starting at one end of the fabric strip, edge stitch the entire length.

7 Fold the bottom hem of the dress back ½" (13mm), press; fold another ½" (13mm) back, press, and pin in place. Topstitch the bottom hem (n).

8 Put the dress on the doll and tie a bow at the neck.

teaching moments

Give your child writing prompts about the Quirky Rag Doll or Jolly Mr. Robot (page 131). Set a timer and allow him or her to free-write a story to read aloud to the rest of the family. Here are some ideas:

- You and your doll/robot join the circus. What would you do?

- You went on a hot air balloon with your doll/robot. Describe what you saw.

- If you and your doll/robot had any superpower, what would it be and why?

jolly mr. robot

Jolly Mr. Robot is a futuristic twist on the classic rag doll, with striped arms and legs, a woolly helmet, and lots of buttons. This oversize toy is perfect for adventures and durable enough to withstand years of affection.

skill level
Take Your Time ☺ ☺ ☺

materials
Basic sewing supplies (page 12)

Jolly Mr. Robot template (page 172)

⅜ yard (34.5cm) of solid-colored wool or cotton for the robot body

Two 6" x 7" (15cm x 18cm) pieces of light-colored fabric for the robot head

¼ yard (23 cm) of striped fabric for the legs and arms

2" x 5" (5cm x 12.5cm) piece of fabric for the robot button box

Two 5" x 6" (12.5cm x 15cm) pieces of wool felt fabric for the robot helmet

Polyester fiberfill

2" x 8" (5cm x 20.5cm) piece of wool felt for the eyes and the helmet's antennae (mix or match colors)

At least 6 buttons, 2 of the same for the eyes

seam allowance
½" (13mm)

finished measurement
22" (56cm) tall

notes
• Use colorful buttons for the body to add personality. Feel free to use more buttons than the amount suggested.

• If this is for a small child (three or under), use small scraps of wool felt in place of buttons to make it safe.

continues

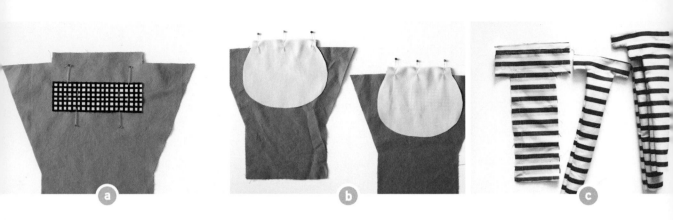

1 Using the template, cut out all the pattern pieces. For the body, cut 2 pieces from the solid fabric. For the head, cut 2 pieces from the light-colored fabric. Cut 4 pieces for the arms and 4 pieces for the legs from the striped fabric. From fabric scraps, cut out the button box for the robot body.

2 Center the button box 1" (2.5cm) down from the top of the body and use a zigzag stitch to appliqué the button box onto the front body fabric (a).

3 With the right sides together, line up the raw edges of the neck to the base of the head, pin in place, and stitch together. Repeat for back body and head pieces (b).

4 Pin two arm pieces with their right sides together, sew around the perimeter, but make sure to leave a 2" (5cm)

opening along the side of the arm. Clip corners, turn, and press. Repeat for the remaining arm.

5 Pin two leg pieces with their right sides together, sew around the perimeter, leaving a 2" (5cm) opening along the side of the leg. Clip corners, turn, and press. Repeat for the remaining leg pieces (c).

6 Place the front body fabric with right side up, place the arms 1" (2.5cm) down from the top and parallel with the top raw edge of the body. Place the legs 1" (2.5cm) from the sides with the raw edges of the fabric lined up (d). Then place the back body fabric with the right side down, sandwiching the arms and legs inside. Pin in place (e) and sew around the entire perimeter of the body and head, leaving a 3" (7.5cm) opening for turning. Clip the corners and curves. Turn right side out and press (f).

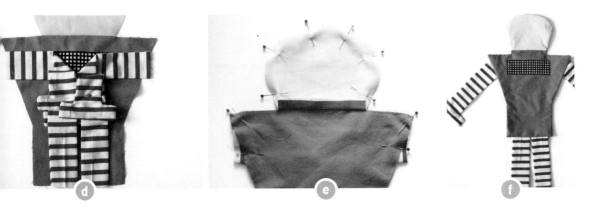

7 Fill the body, arms, and legs with polyester fiberfill and slip stitch all the openings closed.

8 From the wool felt, cut 2 small wool felt circles for the eyes, 2 antenna pieces, and 2 helmet pieces. Cut out an opening from one of the helmet pieces to allow the eyes and face to be seen. Pin the antennae 1" (2.5cm) from the top corners of the helmet and edge stitch around the entire perimeter of the helmet, leaving the base open.

9 Mark the placement of the eyes on the face with an air-fading marker, place the circular wool-felt eyes in their designated spots, and hand-sew a centered X on the circular wool felt pieces to attach them to the head. Hand-sew a button centered on the X for the eyes.

10 Mark the placement for the buttons on the body. Hand-sew each button in its place.

read it together!

The Robot Book
by Heather Brown

The Robot and the Bluebird
by David Lucas

Boy and Bot
by Ame Dyckman

The Three Little Aliens and the Big Bad Robot
by Margaret McNamara

giant dollhouse pillow

This overstuffed pillow takes the classic children's toy to a whole new level of cute. It's not only a home for dolls, but also a fanciful place for naps. Go wild designing a dream house together, using the templates here or your own creative ideas.

skill level
Take Your Time ⊕ ⊕ ⊕

materials
Basic sewing supplies (page 12)

Giant Dollhouse Pillow template (page 173)

1¼ yard (1.1m) blue gingham fabric:

> **22″ x 20″ (56cm x 51cm) piece for the front flap (dollhouse exterior)**
>
> **23½″ x 20″ (59.5cm x 51cm) piece for the interior background**

Three 7½″ x 9″ (19cm x 23cm) pieces of solid-colored fabric for the window pockets

¼ yard (23cm) of fabric for three 7½″ x 6″ (19cm x 15cm) window curtains (mix or match fabrics if desired)

9½″ x 5½″ (24cm x 14cm) piece of solid-colored fabric for the door

Three 7½″ x 1½″ (19cm x 3.8cm) strips of fabric for the window-box planters

Two 9½″ x 9¼″ (24cm x 23.5cm) pieces of fabric for the second-floor rooms (mix or match fabrics if desired)

9½″ x 17½″ (24cm x 44.5cm) piece of fabric for the first-floor room

14″ x 20½″ (35.5cm x 52cm) piece of patterned fabric for the roof front

½ yard (45.5cm) of fabric for the house back

1 yard (0.9m) of fabric for the pillow insert

Two 2″ x 20″ (5cm x 51cm) strips of fabric for the dollhouse straps

Embroidery hoop (optional)

Embroidery thread (optional)

Buttonhole foot

Various buttons, fabric, and wool scraps for decorative purposes

1 yard (0.9m) of interfacing or stabilizer

Free-motion quilting foot

Polyester fiberfill

Five ⅞″ buttons for closures

One ⅜″ button for doorknob

seam allowance
½″ (13mm)

finished measurements
18″ x 35″ (45.5cm x 89cm)

continues

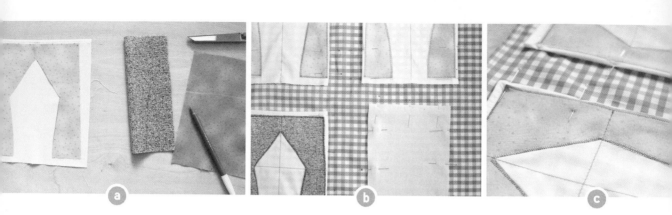

notes

- This is *your* child's dollhouse, so customize it any way you want. Don't confine yourself to the look of this dollhouse, especially when it comes to decorating the inside. If you want to avoid free-motion quilting on the inside, use a solid, light-colored fabric for the inside of the house and allow your child to paint or draw it with fabric markers and fabric paint. When the designs are dry, outline the drawings with a simple running stitch.

- For a simpler pillow, create just the facade of the house, without the interior, by omitting the flap and dollhouse straps, and sewing the pockets on to the outside of the house instead.

This project uses a lot of pieces, so I highly suggest cutting, pressing, and organizing most of the pieces in advance to smoothly transition from one step to another. The back fabric, however, cannot be cut out until the front dollhouse fabric pieces are assembled. The dimensions might vary slightly as the front is pieced together.

house exterior

1 Using the 22" x 20" (56cm x 51cm) front dollhouse exterior fabric (blue gingham), fold the top, bottom, and right edges under ¼" (6mm), press, fold under another ¼" (6mm), press, and pin in place. Topstitch around the 3 folded sides.

2 Using the 7½" x 9" (19cm x 23cm) solid-colored window pocket pieces, fold the top edge under ¼" (6mm), press, fold under another ¼" (6mm), and press. Pin in place and topstitch. Repeat for the remaining 2 window pockets.

3 Cut out three 7½" x 6" (19cm x 15cm) pieces from the window curtain fabric. Cut the curtain 1" (2.5cm) down from the top, 1½" (3.8cm) from the side edge, and 2" (5cm) from the side bottom edge (see diagram opposite). Center the

curtains on the window pockets and appliqué them on (a).

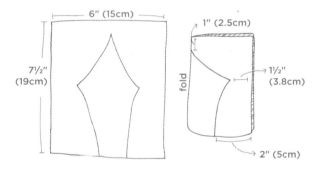

6" (15cm)

7½" (19cm)

fold

1" (2.5cm)

1½" (3.8cm)

2" (5cm)

4 On the front of each window pocket, straight-stitch a line down the center, starting just below the topstitching and ending at the base of the pocket. Proceed to straight-stitch from the center across the window, starting at the edge of the left curtain panel and stopping at the opposite edge of the right curtain panel. This creates the illusion of windowpanes.

5 Mark the placement for the front door with an air-fading marker; it should be 2½" (6.5cm) from the right edge and ½" (13mm) up from the bottom edge (see diagram below). Appliqué it onto the front of the house (b).

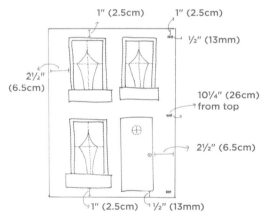

1" (2.5cm)　　1" (2.5cm)

½" (13mm)

2½" (6.5cm)

10¼" (26cm) from top

2½" (6.5cm)

1" (2.5cm)　½" (13mm)

6 Mark the placement of the window pockets on the front fabric with an air-fading marker: 2½" (6.5cm) from the edge, top windows 1" (2.5cm) down from

continues

the top and the bottom window 1" (2.5cm) up from the bottom edge. Fold each side edge of each window-

pocket piece under ¼" (6mm), press, fold under another ¼" (6mm), and press again. Place the pockets with their wrong sides down on the right side of the front fabric in their marked positions and pin in place. Edge stitch both sides of the window in place, leaving the base open (c).

7 Mark the placement for the window-box planters: the top raw edge of the window box should overlap the base of the window by ¼" (6mm); pin in place (d). Appliqué the window boxes onto the base of the window.

8 Make three buttonholes (page 26) on the right side of the front, placed ½" (13mm) from the outer right-hand edges, 1" (2.5cm) from the top and bottom edges, and 10¼" (26cm) from the center hole.

9 Use more buttons, wool, and fabric scraps to add details to the front of the house.

house interior

1 Place the two 9½" x 9¼" (24cm x 23.5cm) second-floor pieces with their right sides together. Make sure all the edges are aligned, pin one of the longer sides together, and stitch in place. Press the seam open.

2 With right sides together, place both long sides of the 9½" x 17½" (24cm x 44.5cm) first-floor room against the long side of the two second-floor rooms. Pin in place and stitch the long sides together (see diagram below). Press the seams open. This is the interior rooms fabric.

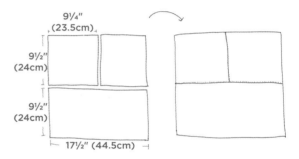

3 Using the interior rooms fabric pieces as a guide, cut out lightweight interfacing or stabilizer. Fuse the stabilizer and the fabric square together.

4 Using the furniture templates (or your own designs), cut out pieces of furniture from fabric and wool felt. Place furniture and pin in place (e). Free-motion quilt (page 24) the house interior and hand-sew any extra details—buttons, wool, or fabric scraps—to the inside of your home. Once done customizing, press the entire house interior. Congratulations! You just completed your first interior design job.

5 Place the front interior fabric with its right side up. Center the interior rooms fabric on top with its right side facing up; it should be placed 3" (7.5cm) from the top and bottom edges, and 1¼" (3cm) from the sides. Pin in place and zigzag-stitch the entire inside fabric on. Stitch in the ditch (page 24) on each seam in the house to define the walls.

6 Cut out the roof fabric. Line up the base of the roof with the top of the front interior fabric with their right sides together, pin in place, and stitch together (see diagram below). Press the seam open.

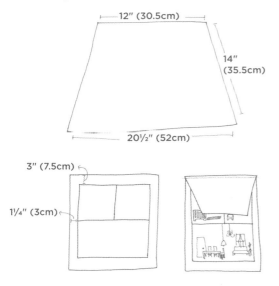

pillow backing

1 Place the front interior fabric (the body with roof attached) on top of the back fabric. Trace the entire perimeter of the house and add an additional 6" (15cm) to the length; cut it out.

2 Mark the center of the backing and cut in half crosswise.

3 On the top half of the back fabric (the portion with the roof), fold one edge of the fabric 1" (2.5cm), press; fold another 2" (5cm), press, pin, and topstitch.

4 Mark the placement for the 2 button-holes: 1" (2.5cm) from the folded edge and 6" (15cm) from the side edge. Sew the buttonholes (see diagram below).

5 With the remaining half of the back fabric, fold under the edge of the fabric 1" (2.5cm), press, fold under another 2" (5cm), press, pin in place, and topstitch.

pillow insert

1 Place the front interior fabric (the body with roof attached) on top of the pillow insert fabric, trace the entire perimeter of the house, and cut out 2 identical pieces.

continues

2 With the right sides of the pillow insert fabric together, sew around the entire perimeter, leaving a 3" (7.5cm) opening for turning. Clip the corners. Turn right side out and press.

3 Stuff the pillow insert with polyester fiberfill to the desired pillow thickness. Slip stitch the opening closed.

dollhouse ties

1 Fold both 2" x 20" (5cm x 51cm) strips of fabric in half lengthwise with their right sides together and press. Using a ¼" (6mm) seam allowance, sew the entire length of the strip. Turn and press.

2 Fold each open end in ¼" (6mm), press, and edge stitch to close. Continue to edge stitch both sides of the strap. Repeat for the second tie.

assembling the dollhouse pillow

1 Lay out all the dollhouse pieces in the following order from bottom to top: front interior fabric piece with its right side facing up, the center of one dollhouse tie 6¼" (16cm) down from the top and another 6¼" (16cm) up from the bottom, the front exterior fabric with its right side facing up and the left-hand raw edges lined up with the left-hand raw edges of the front interior fabric. Fold the remaining half of both dollhouse ties over and line each up with its other half a layer beneath it; repeat for the second house strap. Lay down the top half of the back fabric with its wrong side facing up (make sure the top roof and all raw edges are aligned with the other layers); place the bottom back fabric on top with its wrong side facing up and the bottom raw edge lined up with previous layers. Starting at the center of the pillow, pin in place intermittently to prevent movement while sewing the perimeter. Continue pinning around the entire perimeter of the pillow.

2 Sew around the entire perimeter of the pillow. Clip the corners. Turn right side out through the pillow insert opening and press.

3 Stuff with the pillow insert, mark the placement for the buttons for the front fabric and back fabric, and sew the buttons into place.

read it together!
The Doll People
by Ann M. Martin

Twig
by Elizabeth Orton Jones

The Napping House
by Audrey Wood

Home
by Alex T. Smith

the magic cloth

Kids can make a toy out of anything, as this piece of cloth proves.

Cut out a 30" x 30" (76cm x 76cm) piece of fun, solid fabric, and allow your child to draw or paint on it. To your little one, sometimes it will be a cape, sometimes a head scarf, other times a picnic blanket or a bag. It might even be a doll's swaddling blanket or a flag. A simple piece of fabric can provide countless hours of entertainment.

colorful plaid a-frame tent

Hiding away. Reading a good book. Pretending to be in a castle! All these things can happen under this colorful tent. Once parents have set up the basic frame, kids can create their own masterpiece by weaving strips of fabric together any way they'd like.

skill level
Take Your Time ⓣ ⓣ ⓣ

materials
Basic sewing supplies (page 12)

Four 1" x 3" x 48" (2.5cm x 7.5cm x 122cm) pieces of whitewood molding

Ruler

Pencil

Drill with a ¾" (2cm) spade bit

Two 1" x 3" x 36" (2.5cm x 7.5cm x 91cm) pieces of whitewood molding (optional for use on slippery surfaces, such as hardwood floors)

Three ¾" x 48" (2cm x 122cm) poplar dowels

Two 6" x 45" (15cm x 114cm) pieces of fabric for the bottom panels

Nine 4" x 80" (10cm x 203cm) strips of fabric

Sixteen 4" x 58" (10cm x 147.5cm) strips of fabric

seam allowance
½" (13mm) except where otherwise noted

notes
- The woven cover can also be made without being sewn by omitting the bottom panels and increasing the length of the long strips of fabric. This will allow more room to tie the cover onto the bottom dowels.

- If you would like a more traditional tent cover, a twin-size sheet fits the frame almost perfectly with a bit of trimming to make the fabric exactly 44" x 84" (112cm x 213.5cm).

continues

143

a-frame tent

1 From the top of each of the four 1" x 3" x 48" (2.5cm x 7.5cm x 122cm) pieces of molding, measure 6" (15cm) down and mark with a pencil. With a drill and ¾" (2cm) spade bit, drill a hole at the center of the mark; try to center the hole on the molding. This is the top of the tent frame.

2 From the opposite end of the molding, measure 1½" (3.8cm) down and mark with a pencil. With the drill and the ¾" (2cm) spade bit, drill a hole at the mark; try to center the hole on the molding. These holes will be for the bottom of the A-frame tent.

3 (Optional, see note in step 6.) From the short end of both 1" x 3" x 36" (2.5cm x 7.5cm x 91cm) pieces of whitewood molding, measure in 1"

(2.5cm) and mark with the pencil. With the drill and the ¾" (2cm) spade bit, drill a hole at the pencil mark; try to center the hole as best as possible.

4 Place two 1" x 3" x 48" (2.5cm x 7.5cm x 122cm) pieces of molding on top of each other, making sure the holes are lined up, and push a dowel through the holes of the two pieces of molding. The holes should have a pretty tight grip and keep the dowel in place. Repeat for the other two 1" x 3" x 48" (2.5cm x 7.5cm x 122cm) pieces of molding. This is the top of the A-frame.

5 Insert another dowel through the bottom holes for one side and repeat for the other.

6 If using on a slippery surface such as hardwood floors, insert the remaining shorter moldings (1" x 3" x 36" [2.5cm x 7.5cm x 91cm]) that run across the tent opening on the bottom of the tent, connecting them to the dowels.

note
This prevents the tent from slipping if it will be used on smooth surfaces. If the tent is solely for outside use or on carpeting, skip this step.

tent cover

note
It is best to work on the cover in a large open space where you can lay out all the pieces while you work.

1 Fold the short sides of the bottom panel in ¼" (6mm), press, fold in another ¼" (6mm), and press again. Edge stitch the entire length. Fold the opposite end of the bottom panel in ¼" (6mm), press, fold in another ¼" (6mm), and press again. Edge stitch this second short side. Fold the bottom panels in half lengthwise. Repeat for the second bottom panel.

2 Place ½" (13mm) of one end of each of the nine 4" x 80" (10cm x 203cm) strips of fabric in the bottom panel, spacing them about 1" (2.5cm) apart. Pin in place and edge stitch ¼" (6mm) from the open, folded edge. Repeat for the opposite end of the strips and the second bottom panel (a).

3 Attach the tent cover to the tent frame by inserting the bottom dowels through the bottom panels (b).

4 With your child, weave the sixteen 4" x 58" (10cm x 147.5cm) strips of fabric about 1" (2.5cm) apart through the long strips of the tent cover (c). Do not weave the last 6" (15cm) on each side, allowing it to hang free; these ends will later be tied to the frame of the tent. Pinning each end and overlapping the square in place (d) will help when the strips are sewn together.

5 Remove the tent cover from the frame and edge stitch ½" (13mm) each side length of the tent cover. This joins the vertical and horizontal strips in place.

6 Place the tent cover back on the frame. Straighten out the strips of fabric. Cut the 6" (15cm) of unwoven, hanging fabric in half all the way to the seam, snipping the seam. Use this to pull the tent cover taut onto the tent frame and tie around the molding. Repeat with all the remaining strips (e).

read it together!
Iggy Peck, Architect
by Andrea Beaty

The Three Little Pigs:
An Architectural Tale
by Steven Guarnaccia

Where the Wild Things Are
by Maurice Sendak

Jumanji
by Chris Van Allsburg

let's celebrate!

Special occasions don't require elaborate parties or fancy gifts. Simple and sweet things are always best. For our birthday parties we typically have smaller celebrations. We like to go all out for our baby's first birthday, but after that we're pretty low-key and do what we feel best suits the personality of the birthday girl. Or if she has a special request, we try to make that happen within reason.

Naturally, birthdays aren't the only days to celebrate. In fact, every day should be acknowledged. Gifts can be given "just because," and garlands can be stitched together to make a bedroom or backyard look pretty. Part of the joy of life is finding the beauty in everyday moments. Here, you'll find projects inspired by some of our favorite gifts, party ideas, and seasonal decorations.

Most kids love to decorate, so get them involved in the party prep, too. Even tiny hands can help assemble simple garlands that we can string over the fireplace mantel for holidays. Every birthday, our two oldest girls love making hand-drawn banners and pictures. They go crazy making signs! It might not match the decor I had in mind, but they created it, and when we put it up, they're so proud to see their handmade decorations celebrating the special occasion.

hello sweet banner

Hanging a homespun cross-stitched message in an unexpected place is sure to make someone smile. Customized with any word or phrase you'd like, this little banner introduces basic cross-stitch techniques.

skill level
Sew Quick ⬤

materials
Basic sewing supplies (page 12)

14" x 10" (35.5cm x 25.5cm) piece of burlap

Embroidery hoop

Embroidery floss

³/₁₆" x 16" (5mm x 40.5cm) or smaller dowel

24" (61cm) string or yarn for hanging

finished measurements
14" x 10" (35.5cm x 25.5cm)

notes
• Change the saying on this banner to anything you want! Print out words in your desired font, then create your own cross-stitch pattern following the printout.
• Younger children can create the banner using a blunt tapestry needle or plastic lacing needle.

1 Transfer the pattern to the burlap by dotting the center of each cross-stitched X in each letter on the woven burlap fabric (a).

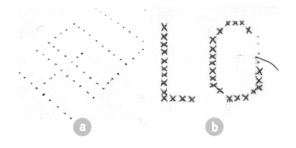

2 Cross-stitch over the dots (page 20). Burlap is easy to use because the warp and weft are evenly spaced; just remember to go over the same number of threads consistently each time you create an X. You can be as traditional as you want by keeping each cross touching each other going in and out of the same hole, or experiment by slightly spacing each X apart (b).

3 Fold the top of the banner down 1½" (3.8cm) and press. Pin in place and topstitch across to make a casing.

4 Insert the dowel through the casing, tie a string to each end of the dowel, and hang!

get groovy garlands

Bunting spruces up any space. Whether for a special occasion or just as an everyday decoration, these mix-and-match banners are the perfect excuse to use up scrap fabrics. Use the two patterns here as inspiration, and customize your own with different shapes.

skill level
Sew Quick ⊚

holiday string lights

These strings of Christmas lights would look especially sweet over a mantel.

materials
Basic sewing supplies (page 12)

Get Groovy Garlands template (page 173)

¼ yard (23cm) total of wool felt in various colors (yields about 16 lightbulbs)

76" (193cm) strand of yarn

Safety pin

Fabric glue

note
Use pastel colors to make decorations for spring.

1 Using the template, cut out as many pattern pieces as desired. You will need 2 pieces per light: the bulb and the light top.

2 Fold the green light top piece in half and insert the flat edge of the lightbulb in ¼" (6mm), pin in place, and topstitch. Repeat for each bulb (a).

3 Using the safety pin on one end of the yarn, string the yarn through each folded-over top, space out each bulb into its desired spot, and add a dab of fabric glue inside the bulb top to attach the yarn. Repeat until all the bulbs have been attached. Cut the string of lights to the desired length (b).

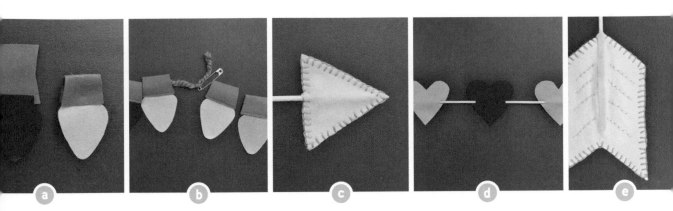

catch the hearts

Cupid shot his arrow and caught a bunch of hearts on it. Sweet enough for Love Day—or any day.

materials

Basic sewing supplies (page 12)

Get Groovy Garlands template
  (page 173)

⅛ yard (11.5cm) of wool felt
  (use different colors for the hearts
  and the arrow)

³⁄₁₆″ x 36″ (5mm x 91cm) dowel

Glue gun and glue

Embroidery floss

40″ (101.5cm) strand of string or yarn

note
Add more hearts, change the template size, or make a garland of all arrows.

1 Using the template, cut out all the pieces from wool felt: 2 for the arrow point, 2 for the arrow end, and 5 hearts.

2 Sandwich the dowel between the two arrow points, and add a dab of glue at the base of the wool felt pieces to secure the dowel and wool felt together. Using an embroidery needle and floss, blanket stitch (page 19) the point together (c).

3 Cut a ¼″ (6mm) slit on each side of a heart and thread it on the dowel. Repeat for the remaining hearts (d).

4 Sandwich the end of the dowel with the two felt arrow end pieces. Then add a dab of glue at the base of the wool felt pieces to secure the dowel and the wool felt together. Blanket stitch around and use a running stitch (page 19) to make 4 lines on each side to further enhance the design (e).

5 Cut a string to the desired length, attach it to the ends of the wooden dowel, and hang it up!

no-sew

no-sew bunting

This is even more fun than your traditional bunting because you don't need to sew anything!

materials

No-Sew Bunting template
(page 174)

1 yard (0.9m) of cotton fabric
(yields about 15–18 bunting pieces)

note
Create a garland based on your favorite story by painting on each shape in the bunting.

1 Using the triangle or rounded square template, cut out the pattern from various fabrics (a).

2 Arrange the pieces into the preferred order. Knot each arm piece together for the desired length of garland (b).

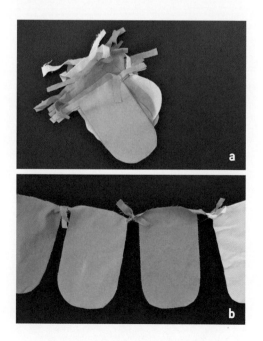

smart party bags

Why use plastic bags to hold party goodies when they will just be cast off into the trash? These chalk-cloth bags are perfect for holding colorful favors and can be drawn on again and again.

skill level
Sew Quick ☺

materials
Basic sewing supplies (page 12)

Smart Party Bags template (page 174)

½ yard (45.4cm) of chalk cloth (makes 4 bags)

Rolling sewing foot (for sewing on chalk cloth)

Hole punch

36" (91cm) length of suede cording or yarn for each bag

Chalk

seam allowance
¼" (6mm)

finished measurements
7½" x 8" (19cm x 20.5cm) without strap

notes
- The decorating possibilities for this project are endless. Use a bit of glue and buttons, pom-poms (page 33), or jewels to fit your party theme.
- The bag can also be made from cotton fabric, wool felt, or vinyl.

1 Cut out the pouch pieces from chalk cloth using the template: 1 front piece, 1 back piece.

2 With their wrong sides together, sew around the bag, leaving the top open.

3 Punch out a hole on each top corner of the bag through the front and back about ½" (13mm) down from the top and ½" (13mm) in from the side.

4 Cut the suede cording or yarn. Insert each length of the cording through the holes on one side and knot securely. Repeat for the second set of holes.

5 Use chalk to decorate the bags! They can be personalized with each child's name ahead of time, or make decorating the bags an activity during the party.

boom boom party drum

These little friends make great party wands and noisemakers. Have them ready for the party, or let kids make them at the party.

materials

Small screwdriver or other object that can poke a small hole

3"- (7.5cm-) wide round papier-mâché box

Paints and paintbrushes

$^{15}/_{16}$" (16mm) foam ball

Glue gun and glue sticks

$^3/_{16}$" x 12" (5mm x 30.5cm) wooden dowel

11" (28cm) piece of twine

Plastic lacing needle (optional)

Two $^3/_4$" (2cm) wooden beads

1 Use the screwdriver to poke a hole, centered on the side of the round box; poke another hole in the side directly across from the first. Poke a third hole, again centered, at the bottom.

2 Paint faces on the round container. Make two different faces or make them the same. Allow them to dry completely (a).

3 Glue the foam ball inside the top center (opposite the third, bottom hole). Add a bit more glue to the bottom of the foam ball, insert the dowel through the bottom hole, and then insert the dowel into the foam ball to set it in place. Let the glue dry.

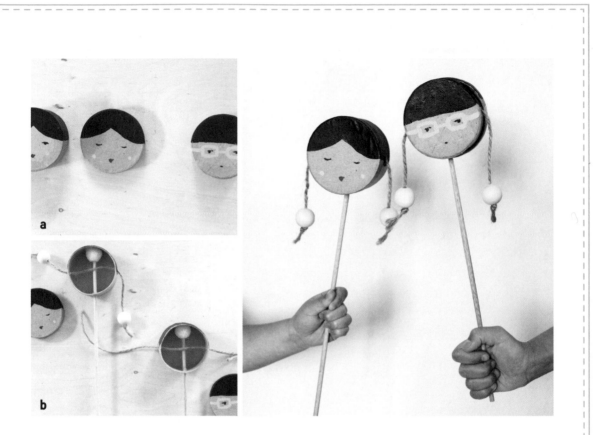

4 Insert the twine through one side hole and out of the second hole. A lacing needle may help pull it through, depending on the size of the hole.

5 Insert a wooden bead into each end of the twine and knot both ends (b).

6 Attach the box's lid and glue to secure it in place. Make sure the twine is hanging evenly on each side, turn the dowel, and have fun!

the "you" book

You are special! You know that, right? Well, why not spread the love with this fabric book—use it to tell a story, document a memorable event, or tell someone all the reasons you love him or her. It's the perfect place to try out all the techniques we've learned together and use leftover fabrics from your other projects.

skill level

Sew Quick ☺

materials

Basic sewing supplies (page 12)

Four 7½" x 18" (19cm x 45.5cm) pieces of light-colored cotton fabric

Fabric markers or fabric paint and paintbrushes

seam allowance

½" (13mm)

finished measurements

6½" x 8½" (16.5cm x 21.5cm) when book is closed

notes

- This can be a book of pictures, a short story, or a touch-and-feel book with interesting fabrics and notions.
- Make this in any size of your choosing; just be sure to add 1" (2.5cm) to all the sides to account for the seam allowances.
- Try the following prompts to inspire the book's author:

  You make my day brighter when . . .
  You're as sweet as a . . .
  You're special to me because . . .

continues

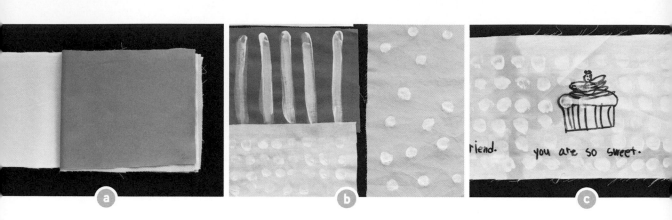

1 With the wrong sides together, pair the pages of the book together, and fold them in half crosswise. With an air-fading marker, mark the corner of each book starting with the top: cover, page 1, page 2, page 3, page 4, page 5, page 6, and back (a).

2 Have your child paint background designs on the fabric. Allow the design to dry completely and press to heat-set it (b).

3 Lay out all the pages and, with an air-fading marker, mark where the fold of the book will be.

4 Discuss the sayings you both would like to be written in your book and have your child write them out and draw a corresponding picture. Allow the design to dry completely and press to heat-set it (c).

5 Place the pair of pages with their right sides together; double-check to make sure they are in the correct order. The cover and back are paired with pages 1 and 6. Pages 2 and 5 are paired with pages 3 and 4. Sew down the entire length of the top and bottom long edges. Leave the short side open for turning. Turn right side out and press. Repeat for the remaining pair of fabric pages (d).

read it together!

**Guess How Much
I Love You**
by Sam McBratney

The Important Book
by Margaret Wise Brown

I Love You Forever
by Robert Munsch

6 Place the book pages in order, fold them in half, and tuck open ends in ½" (13mm). Press and pin in place. Continue to tuck in the remaining pages to line up with the previous page (e).

note
The outer pages are slightly wider in order to cover the inner pages.

7 Edge stitch the short side of each page ¼" (6mm) from the folded edge.

8 Open up the pages and edge stitch the long side of each page ¼" (6mm) from the edge.

9 Fold the book pages in half again; be sure pages of the book are aligned. Press the folded book and edge stitch ¼" (6mm) from the fold (f). This creates the spine of the book.

go on a scavenger hunt

Scavenger hunts are just plain fun, so why not plan one for the family to go on (or send Dad on one with the kids for Father's Day)? Prepare a simple list of ten things, share it with the children, and then go out to find them. Kids can get creative about what fits the criteria. If you have a camera, take a picture of each item you find on the list and make a little book of your adventure. Invent your own list, or use this one to get you started:

1. Totally rocks	6. Sky blue
2. Pink and frilly	7. Giant robot
3. Roses are red	8. Happy faces
4. Flying high	9. Party animals
5. Heavily striped	10. Lots of love

toss the tail on the bear

Are your kids up for a little competition? A spin on Pin the Tail on the Donkey, this game calls for good aim to toss the tail onto the bear. Kids will not only love lining up to play, but the bear could also be used as a blanket or a rug for reading. Multipurpose projects like this are my fave!

skill level
Make in an Afternoon ☺ ☺

materials
Basic sewing supplies (page 12)

Toss the Tail on the Bear template (page 174)

1¼ yards (1.1m) of fabric for the top

1¼ yards (1.1m) of fabric for the back

1¼ yards (1.1m) of cotton batting

Wool felt scraps for the cheeks and tail

Fabric scraps for the ears

Fabric scraps at least 6" (15cm) square for the beanbags

Fabric paint and paintbrushes or sponges

Embroidery floss for attaching the cheeks and tail

Embroidery hoop (optional)

½ cup of dried beans per beanbag

seam allowance
½" (13mm)

finished measurements
Bear is 32" x 40" (81cm x 101.5cm)

Each beanbag is 4" x 4" (10cm x 10cm)

notes
- If this is going to be used as a game, the tail needs to stand out on the bear, so use a contrasting color felt or fabric piece.
- Instead of a game, the bear could be a giant softie or floor cushion by just omitting the cotton batting and stuffing it with polyester fiberfill instead.

continues

notes *(continued)*
- Feel free to use a patterned fabric for the top of the bear instead of painting a pattern.

1 Cut out all the necessary fabric pieces using the templates: the top bear panel, back bear panel, and cotton batting; 6 ear pieces (2 front ear fabric, 2 back ear fabric, 2 cotton batting pieces); 2 rosy cheeks; and 1 bear tail.

read it together!

"Why the Bear Has a Short Tail," in
The Book of Nature Myths
by Florence Holbrook

Brown Bear, Brown Bear, What Do You See?
by Bill Martin

Goldilocks and the Three Bears
by James Marshall

2 Paint the bear face and body. Allow them to dry completely and press to heat-set.

3 To layer the ear, place the two ear pieces with their right sides together, and place the cotton batting piece on top. Pin in place and stitch around, leaving the base of the ear open. Clip all curves and corners. Turn and press. Repeat for the remaining ear.

4 With an air-fading marker, on the front bear panel, mark the placement for the ear.

5 Fold the base of the ear in 1/2" (13mm), press, and pin it in place on the front bear panel. Edge stitch as close to the fold as possible. Repeat for the remaining ear (a).

6 Hand-sew on the rosy cheeks and the bear tail using a running stitch.

note
An embroidery hoop always helps when hand-sewing layers onto fabric.

7 To assemble the bear, place the cotton batting down first, next place the front and back body panels on top with their right sides together. Pin all the layers together and topstitch around the entire bear body, leaving a 3"–4" (7.5cm–10cm) opening for turning (b). Clip all the curves around the body. Turn and press.

8 Slip stitch the opening close.

beanbags

1 Using the template, cut out 2 pieces of fabric per beanbag (c).

2 With right sides together, stitch around the perimeter, leaving a 2" (5cm) opening for turning. Clip the curves around the circle, turn, and press.

3 Fill the beanbags with beans and slip stitch the opening closed. To avoid any hand-sewing, just fold in the opening, press, and edge stitch as close to the folded edge as possible.

party ideas

Sometimes it's just plain fun to throw a party. It doesn't even have to be someone's birthday; you can host one just because. Here are some fun party ideas to fire up your imagination:

- **Storybook Soiree:** Pick a story to plan a party around. We chose "Goldilocks and the Three Bears" when my oldest turned three. We ate porridge, the girls made bear softies, and there were lots of different chairs.

- **Pie Contest:** Make it a bit more competitive and have a cash prize. This saves you from having to make dessert, because everyone else is bringing it.

- **Dance Party:** Find a friend to teach a group of kids a dance. Make a craft and enjoy some snacks. When the parents come back to pick up their kids, treat them to a special performance.

- **Breakfast Bash:** Most parties are in the afternoon on the weekend. But hosting a breakfast party lets guests enjoy some treats to celebrate, then go on their merry way with the afternoon to take care of other things.

teaching moments

Have your child write his or her own story of how his or her bear got its short tail and draw an accompanying picture.

resources

All the projects in this book call for materials that are readily available at your local craft stores. The following list of suppliers will help you find all the materials you need to complete the projects in the book. If you have trouble finding a product, consult the websites listed to locate a distributor.

Fabrics used in the book range from vintage to store-bought (some long ago) and hand-painted or hand-drawn designs, so keep in mind that you might not be able to re-create the exact design. The wonderful thing about collaborative sewing is coming up with something you love with your child. All the projects in the book are infused with our personalities, and now it's your turn to make your own works of art.

Homemade Sewing Cards (page 34)
> Plastic sewing needle from Oriental Trading Company
> www.orientaltrading.com

Barrette Baubles (page 51)
> French barrettes from Trim Weaver
> www.trimweaver.com

Silly, Silly Cuckoo Clock (page 105)
> Battery-operated clock arms from Clock Parts
> www.clockparts.com

Hanging Chalkboard, Big Box Theater Troupe, Colorful Plaid A-frame Tent (pages 91, 119, and 143)
> Molding and dowels from Lowes
> www.lowes.com or check your local hardware store

Hanging Chalkboard, Smart Party Bags (pages 91 and 155)
> Chalk cloth from Oil Cloth Addict
> www.etsy.com/shop/oilclothaddict

Fabric
Purl Soho
> www.purlsoho.com/purl

Sew Mama Sew
> www.sewmamasew.com

Sewing supplies, including fabric markers and paint
Amazon
> www.amazon.com

Joann
> www.joann.com

sweetly sketch & tie
reversible frock
ENLARGE BY 440%

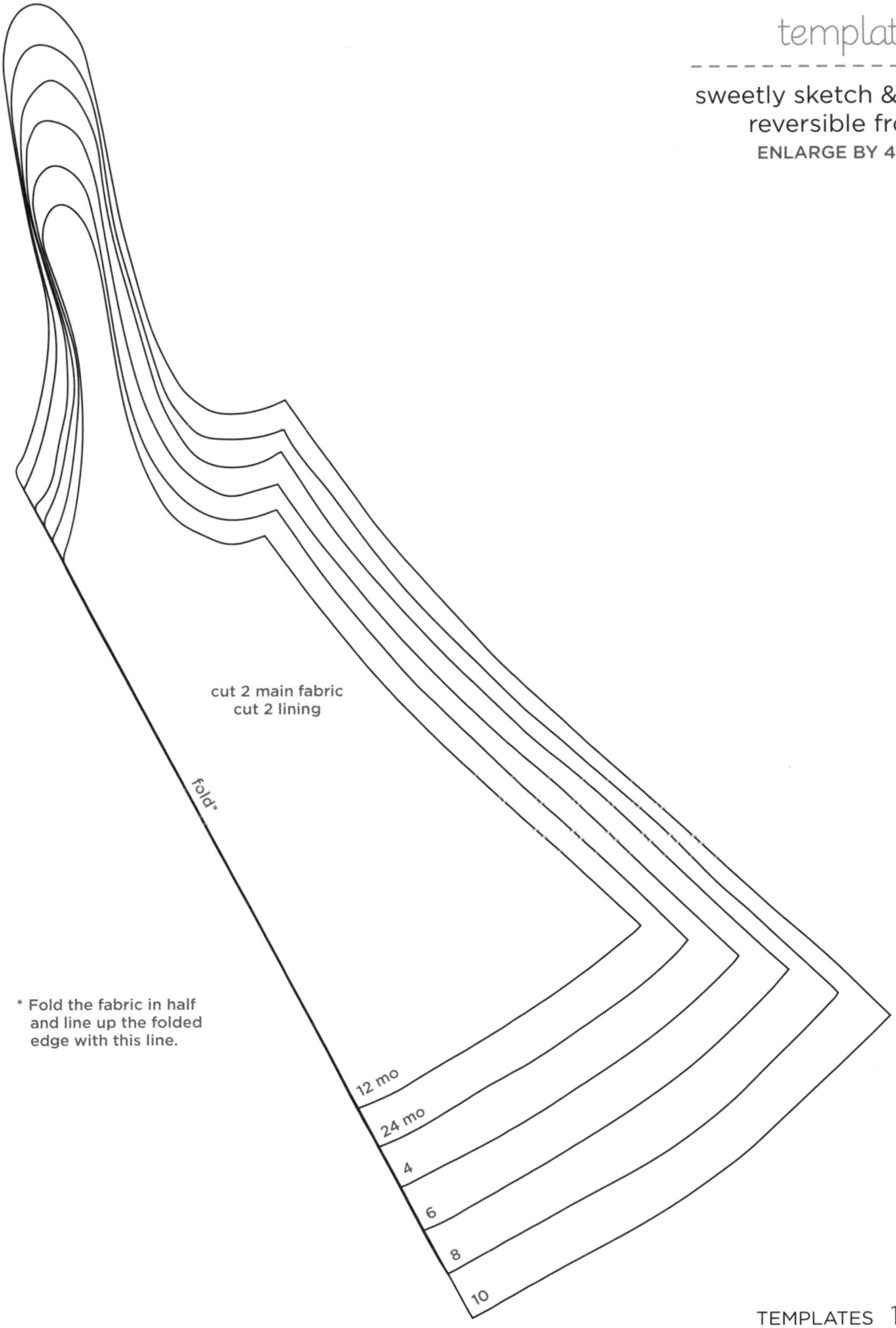

cut 2 main fabric
cut 2 lining

fold*

* Fold the fabric in half
and line up the folded
edge with this line.

12 mo

24 mo

4

6

8

10

running in the sun
shorts
ENLARGE BY 330%

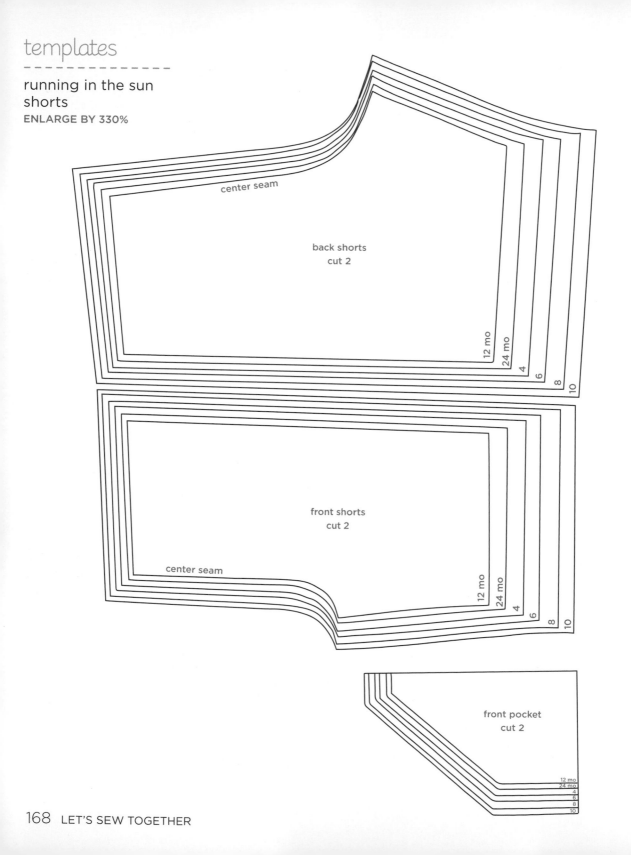

center seam

back shorts
cut 2

12 mo
24 mo
4
6
8
10

front shorts
cut 2

center seam

12 mo
24 mo
4
6
8
10

front pocket
cut 2

12 mo
24 mo
4
6
8
10

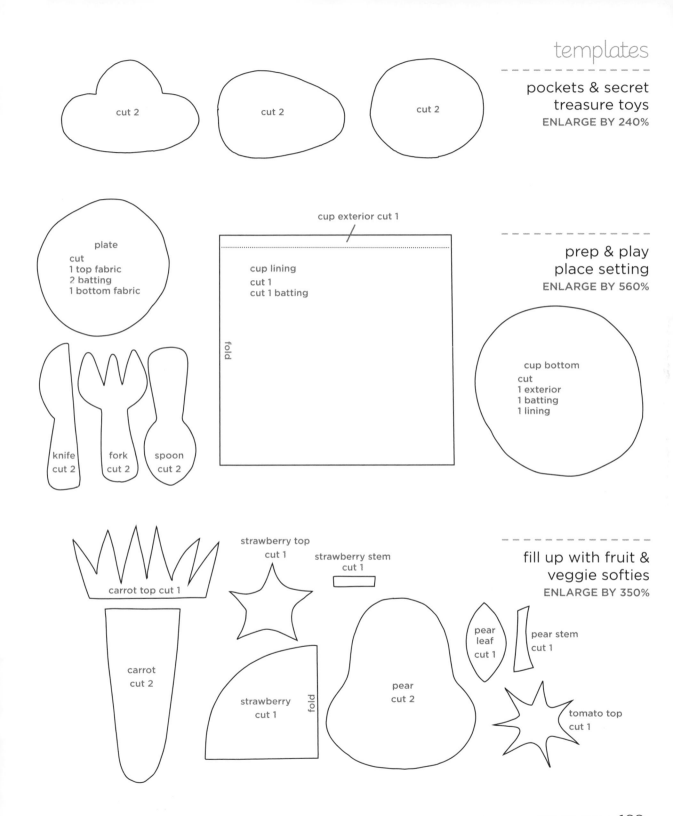

pockets & secret
treasure toys
ENLARGE BY 240%

cut 2

cut 2

cut 2

plate
cut
1 top fabric
2 batting
1 bottom fabric

cup exterior cut 1

cup lining
cut 1
cut 1 batting

fold

prep & play
place setting
ENLARGE BY 560%

cup bottom
cut
1 exterior
1 batting
1 lining

knife
cut 2

fork
cut 2

spoon
cut 2

carrot top cut 1

strawberry top
cut 1

strawberry stem
cut 1

fill up with fruit &
veggie softies
ENLARGE BY 350%

carrot
cut 2

strawberry
cut 1

fold

pear
cut 2

pear
leaf
cut 1

pear stem
cut 1

tomato top
cut 1

templates

- - - - - - - - - - - - - -

travel the world quilt
ENLARGE BY 770%

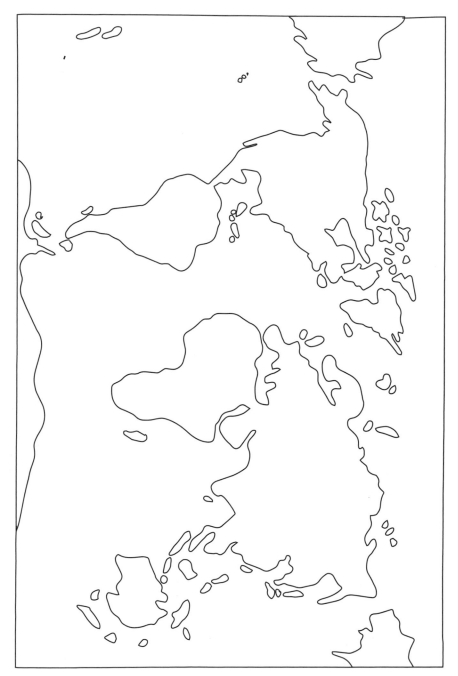

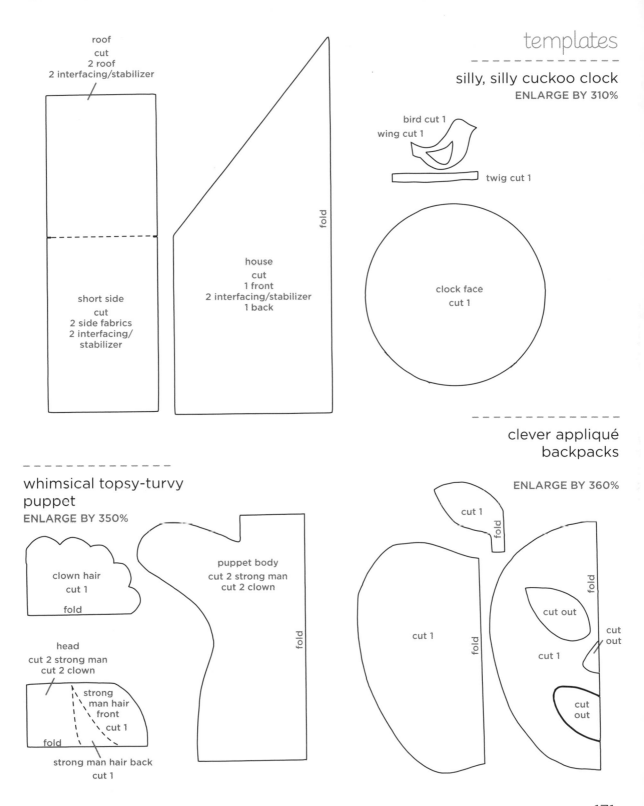

roof
cut
2 roof
2 interfacing/stabilizer

short side
cut
2 side fabrics
2 interfacing/
stabilizer

house
cut
1 front
2 interfacing/stabilizer
1 back

fold

silly, silly cuckoo clock
ENLARGE BY 310%

bird cut 1
wing cut 1
twig cut 1

clock face
cut 1

clever appliqué
backpacks

ENLARGE BY 360%

cut 1
fold

cut 1

fold

cut out

cut
out

cut 1

cut out

whimsical topsy-turvy
puppet
ENLARGE BY 350%

clown hair
cut 1

fold

puppet body
cut 2 strong man
cut 2 clown

fold

head
cut 2 strong man
cut 2 clown

strong
man hair
front
cut 1

fold

strong man hair back
cut 1

templates

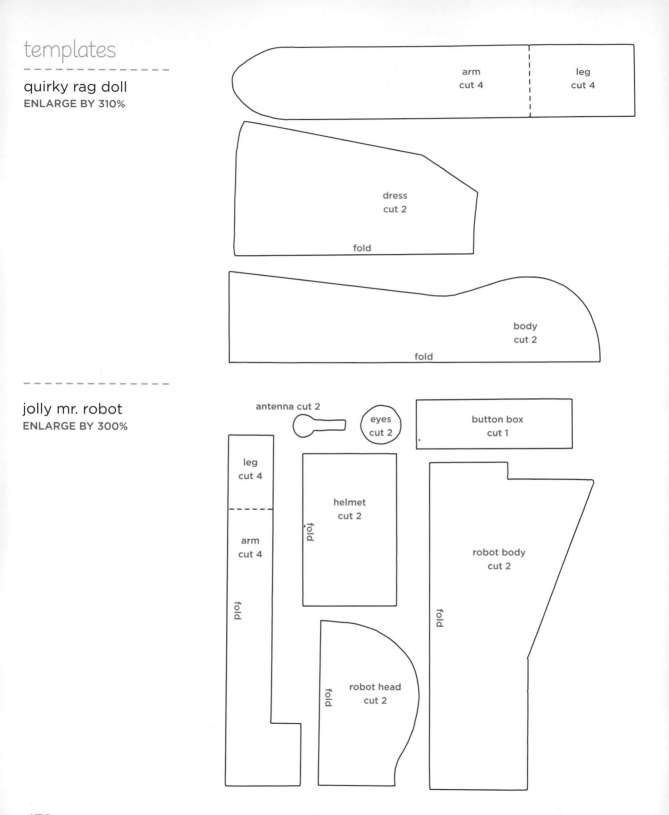

quirky rag doll
ENLARGE BY 310%

arm
cut 4

leg
cut 4

dress
cut 2

fold

body
cut 2

fold

jolly mr. robot
ENLARGE BY 300%

antenna cut 2

eyes
cut 2

button box
cut 1

leg
cut 4

helmet
cut 2

fold

arm
cut 4

fold

robot body
cut 2

fold

fold

robot head
cut 2

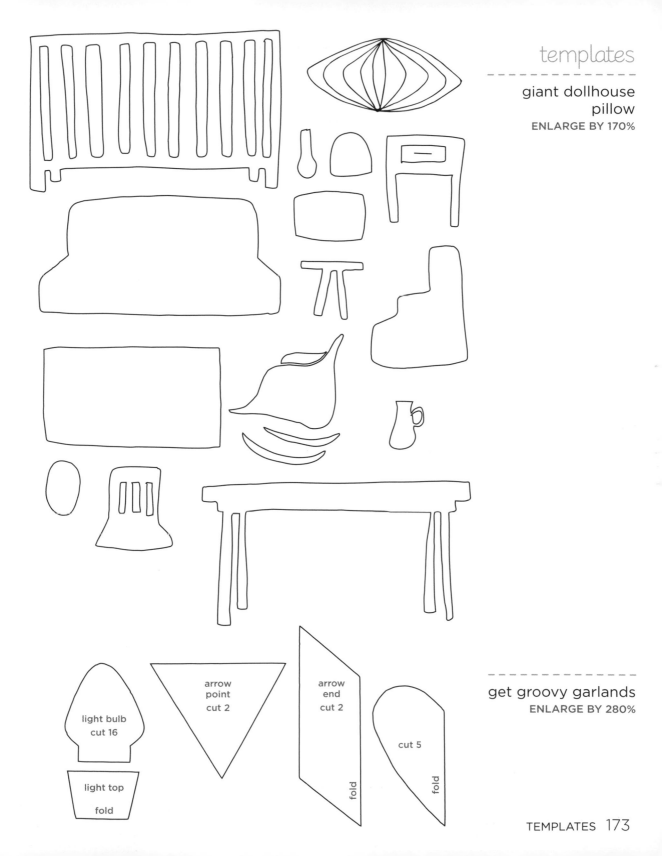

giant dollhouse
pillow
ENLARGE BY 170%

get groovy garlands
ENLARGE BY 280%

light bulb
cut 16

light top

fold

arrow
point
cut 2

arrow
end
cut 2

fold

cut 5

fold

templates

no-sew bunting
ENLARGE BY 430%

toss the tail on the bear
ENLARGE BY 600%

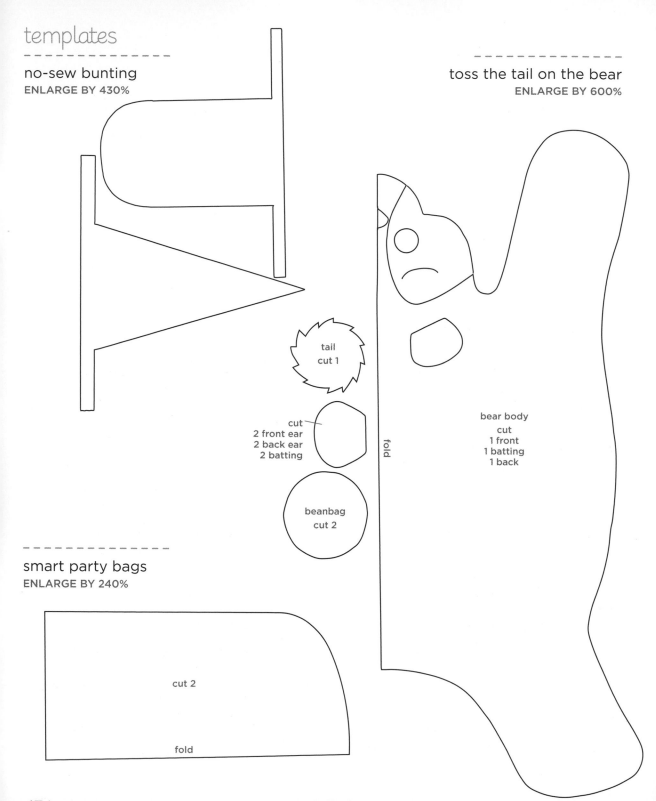

tail
cut 1

cut
2 front ear
2 back ear
2 batting

fold

bear body
cut
1 front
1 batting
1 back

beanbag
cut 2

smart party bags
ENLARGE BY 240%

cut 2

fold

acknowledgments

Life's full of surprises, and no one is more surprised by this book than I am. All I ever wanted was to be a mom, and once that happened, my girls opened up a whole world of inspiration and possibilities.

GIRLS, your love for creating and imagination keeps me wanting to make things for you. I love you.

BEN, thank you for using up all your vacation days and being Mr. Mom on those days when I checked out and sat at the computer or sewing machine for hours on end. You know I loved you from the very first day I met you. No joke. You make my heart go pitter-patter every day.

MOM AND DAD, thank you for providing an environment where imagination was encouraged and following my heart was a must. I get all of this from you. I love you *very* much.

DEAR SIBLINGS, thank you for letting me try out all my ideas on you growing up. You let me dress you up, teach you dances, and boss you around. It's shaped who I am today. Ryan, that paper-bag Ninja Turtle doll I made you that was held together by staples and stuffed with cotton balls will always be one of my proudest creations.

HEY BFF! Thank you for being the second mama to my girls when I needed to get work done and for always letting me boss you around. God grew both of us so much during this whole book thing (more than we ever thought possible); you know I will always be here to point you back to the Christ, so thank you for always doing the same for me. Let's go get BFF necklaces now!

MAMA, thank you for always being so enthusiastic about all my endeavors and flying out here to spoil all of us with your presence so that I could get some work done during the homestretch. You totally helped me meet my deadline! You're the best mother-in-law a gal could ask for!

ANA! Oh my world! You are heaven-sent. Thank you for taking the time to look over my projects and giving them love and attention just like they were your own.

HEATHER, the awesome-saved-my-brain-when-it-was-fried stylist, your ideas are always genius. You totally rock, my friend!

STEPHANIE, you are the best babysitter ever! I could not have gotten any work done if it wasn't for you. You are so much better for my girls than cartoons.

DEAR CAITLIN, the world's best editor! This is as much your baby as it is mine. You found me, and we've both been working on this since November 2011 to make it happen, and it's really happening. Thank you!

TO MY AGENT, Lindsay, thank you for going in and sealing the deal. I never thought in a million years I would have an agent, but I'm glad it's you. You totally get the job done.

THANK YOU TO MY CROSSVIEW FAMILY who prayed for me as I worked on this enormous project. God definitely answered.

TO MY FRIENDS who contributed in advice, encouragement, or a helping hand: Helen, Frances, Melody, Karen, Danni, Jane, Angie, Owen, Nina, Kim (and Andre). Ben says I have too many friends, but I think that's a really good problem to have. You each have had a special role in my life (and in the making of this book), and I'm thankful for you.

TO MY INTERNET PALS who knew what I was working on behind the scenes and encouraged me through this: Rachel, Elsie, Emma, Nathalie, and Bethany. Your little emails of encouragement mean so much! I love being nerdy about crafting with all of you.

TO ALL MY BLOG READERS, you are all totally a part of this, too. Because you pay attention, so did Potter Craft. Thank you for finding our little corner of the Internet interesting and for putting up with all my pictures and ramblings. I'm thankful for you more than you know. I have my arms wrapped around my computer screen right now (really!), giving you all a big, giant hug!

LASTLY, PRAISE THE LORD JESUS! Lord, I'm not sure how you're going to use this to further your kingdom, but that's what I'm praying for.

index